ISBN 1-9009 13-04-6 Paperback
ISBN 1-9009 13-05-4 Hardback

A CIP catalogue for this book is available from the British Library.

First published in 2000 by
Justin Nelson Productions Ltd.,
151 Foxrock Park, Dublin 18.

Printed by Kilkenny People Printing Ltd
Purcellsinch Industrial Estate,
Kilkenny.

Contents

Preface

This is a little book of events surrounding my mother's dying, a time of loss for our family, but also a time of grace. The *real-time* span of the book is only eight months, in the year of '97 – but in what one author calls *'time out of mind'*, it goes back more than a century.

When I was making my pilgrimage back to my mother's childhood, I decided to go farther back to see what I could find out about her father Séamus Duggan and her mother Brigid. Then I needed to explain a bit about my father's family, the McFaddens, and how my dad and mother met and raised seven of us children who are all still alive.

The title of the book, *Coming Safely Home*, was suggested by my friend Beverly Flynn of Chicago. It is a title that reflects the metaphor through which my mother viewed the world. For that reason, it is dedicated to all mothers, so that they might know how precious their love is, and that they might teach their children how to *come safely home* from the pilgrimage of life. It is also dedicated to those caught in the thicket of the journey, who cannot find their homing instincts on life's way.

Stonehill College
Easton, Massachusetts
St. Valentine's Day, 2000 AD

The townland I loved so well

The whole countryside has been to see her now.

In the Rosses of Donegal where I was born, people need no invitation to come to our house. Nor do they bother to call ahead. It is just the custom of country people, and it has always been this way in my lifetime, and before.

There has been a steady stream of visitors from the time my mother took ill after Christmas until now. They say they just want to ask about *Maggie,* as she is known to them, but my sister Margaret brings them into the bedroom to see her anyway. The reason she brings them into the room is, quite simply, that Maggie would not be pleased if anyone who took the trouble to come to visit her were turned away. If she is awake, she greets her visitors with a handshake and thanks them for coming to see her. She may talk to them a little, if she is not too weak.

My brother Jim, who lives in London but who is home just now, thinks it crazy to let all the visitors in to see her. He says the exertion involved will kill her. However, as I reminded Jim, we are not in charge of visiting policy, and it is obvious that Maggie is not saving herself - nor being saved - for the future. This is, for the many who come, *the season of the unspoken goodbye.*

At first, it was the neighbours who came, and then relatives and friends from farther away. Where we live, it is hard to say who is a neighbour and who is not, because the little townlands have no boundaries. One place merges so easily into another, and the situation is not helped by the fact that the Irish had one name for places, and the British imposed another - or a bad transliteration - when they were doing their colonial ordinance surveys in the century before last.

We live in a place called Calhame, and our house is halfway up the last *brae* (hill) on the coast road, before the road turns right to Carrickfinn Airport. Our house is also a hundred yards from an estuary of the Atlantic Ocean; the tides from the ocean fill the estuary twice every twenty-four hours, each tide always forty-five minutes later than the previous one.

When the tide is out, one can see a long strand of silver-gray sand with all manners of pools and tidal streams that are called *deáns* (djaans) in Gaelic. There is an island in the estuary, and rocks covered with sea-wrack and mussels. There are crabs too, wedged tightly into the hard places where they make scraping noises with their carpaces – putting children on notice that they cannot be dislodged with thin sallyrod sticks. The crabs will venture out on their spindly legs only when the tide is coming in. They always seem to be off-balance. Perhaps it is because they are not sure – like some people I know - whether they are walking straight or not.

Below the sand, there are cockles and large clams, which come to the surface to feed off the incoming tide. If you walk against the tide you can quickly spot the dozens of glinty eyes and dark clam pods that cover the sea floor. A quick finger is all that is necessary to dislodge the cockles. The clams can retreat faster and deeper, so they have to be dug up when the tide is out. As children, we spent hundreds of heuristic hours exploring the bounty of our backdoor aquarium.

*　　*　　*　　*

Some of our neighbours live down in The Point - *An Phuinte* in Irish - which used to be quite a distance from our house. Many of the people who would have come to see my mother are now dead, so their sons and daughters come instead – friendly and solicitous as if they were on a solemn pilgrimage. The people from the Point are good people and I daresay for them it is a journey of virgilian *pietas,* almost as strong as if it were to one of their own parents.

They were once my father's customers, and now they are my brother Hugh's customers. Some are Protestant and some Catholic, and they are all equally faithful in their friendship with our family. The Protestants worship in St. Andrews, a small chapel conveniently located in the center of the island. Locally, it is referred to as *The Kirk.* Because of our turbulent history, the word Kirk can denote building, nationality, and religion, all at the same time.

Local history holds that the Carrickfinn Protestants really should be known as *Dissenters* because it was from Henry VIII's brand of the Reformation that they sought refuge. And it was from Scottish shores their ancestors fled – the *Alcorns,* the *Boyds,* the *Fosters* and the *Givens* – all in small boats, looking for freedom in the most unlikely places, among poor, coastland Irish Catholics.

But then, they did not have a great choice of destinations, given the size of their craft and the point of departure. Donegal may have seemed a better choice than the Shetlands or the Faeröes. Or maybe, like some of our modern boat people, they did not know where they would come ashore. But that is how they came to settle on the Donegal coast. They lived in peace with their neighbours, and their neighbours lived in peace with them. We never knew the bitterness of our divided neighbours in the North.

One of the Boyds of New Zealand maintains that his ancestors were given lands in Donegal because they fought in the Williamite wars. This seems hard to sustain, considering that William Boyd, the

Fourth Earl of Kilmarnock, fought with Prince Charles Stuart at Culloden in 1745, was taken prisoner, and lost his head in the Tower of London the following year. This would be more than a half century *after* James II and William of Orange carried their wars to Ireland.

*   *   *   *

Bonnie Charlie' s noo awa
Safely o'er the friendly main,
Mony a hert will brek in twa
Should he ne'er come back again

Will ye no' come back again?
Will ye no' come back again?
Better lo'ed ye canna' be
Will ye no' come back again

There was always a great deal of poverty in our area of Donegal - a hardscrabble place to begin with - carved into great bays and headlands by the glaciers of the last Ice Age. The poverty became more pronounced during World War II, largely because the men and women of the area were not as free to come and go to Scotland to earn a living. This may have been aggravated by Ireland's neutrality during the war, but others say the wolf-packs of Nazi U-boats also played a part. There was also, for young Irish males, the threat of conscription into the British Armed Forces.

Whatever the reason, the scarcity of goods made rationing inevitable. Nothing was left untouched: flour, oatmeal, kerosene, butter and sugar, bacon and sausages, wool and canned goods. Imports of tea were limited and citrus fruit vanished for a period of close to ten years. Even the barnyard was affected: maize stopped coming from America along with the linseed meal that was needed for young calves. The cows got only bran and oats - and pollard in the winter. The hens and pigs got anything that was going. Petrol was always scarce and almost impossible to obtain at certain times. Even Carter's Little Liver Pills deserted the shelves for a while.

As a family we were lucky, because my parents had opened a shop in the village before I was born. My father Jimmy was always very good to his regular customers, and even to those who were not his customers. These were the hardier souls, mostly women, who made the rounds of various stores to see if they could find something *extra* for their children.

Jimmy always found some way to go over the limit to help the poorer families who relied on the gathering of shellfish - or *duilisc* and *carrigeen moss* - to supplement the small amount of income that came from fishing. It may have been some extra flour or sugar, or the prized Darjeeling tea, a pot of jam – but he always came up with something beyond the rations and beyond a mother's expectations. Jimmy had an added worry with some of his customers, for while they came every week, and had the cost of their groceries listed in their book, they had no money to pay. As they say in Ireland, they were *on tick*.

Maggie also tended shop and she was also engaged in this good but trying task of complying with rationing laws - and then trying to go beyond. Besides that, when dad had to be firm with customers whose line of credit was getting longer every week - and no money in the offing - some of the more enterprising mothers used to come to the kitchen to talk to Maggie. She was a mother before all else - she was a soft touch and they knew it. At an opportune moment, Maggie would go down to the shop, and when dad was busy she would put a loaf of bread and some other items under her pinny, and go back up to the kitchen to deliver them – another bout of *tic-de-la-rue* for the finances of the shop.

I am sure there were times when there was not enough money in the till to pay the commercial travelers. And my guess is that, at other times, Maggie borrowed from her father and dad perhaps took loans from his brothers. My brother Hugh remarked recently that it was the parents - for whom most was done – whose children never came around to our shop afterwards. He said this with no malice or rancor, but simply noted it as a fact of life. There is the story of ten lepers cured but only one, a Samaritan, returns to give thanks. Maybe the proportion holds true in all deeds of kindness - and we never notice it - because those who are truly generous do not keep a tally of their giving.

When containers of cigarettes arrived, my brother John and myself took to hoarding a fairly large number of cartons for consumption later in the month. We were the only two in the family small enough at that time to squeeze through the narrow entrances to the attic above the shop. Everyone seemed oblivious to what we were doing, but we took a portion of every brand: *Player's, Capstan, Sweet Afton, Goldflake, Craven A, Player's Weights* and *Woodbine.* Player's Weights were in packs of five for those who could not afford more. I think the Woodbine cigarettes were made from the leftovers of tobacco; they were cheaper to buy, and they appealed to certain smokers. Anyway, at that stage of the war, people would smoke anything.

At month's end we would produce our hoard, in separate packs, for our favourite people when they were in the throes of nicotine withdrawal. We did not know what nicotine withdrawal was at the time, but we observed its effects - along with the yellowed fingers that smoked a fag to its burning butt-end. We had never heard of the Mafia either, but we had heard of the black market, and as far as our shop went, *we were it.*

*   *   *   *

Some of the women came up from the Point, barefoot and carrying bags of periwinkles or mussels on their backs. They usually walked up the strand when the tide was out; that way it was shorter and easier on their feet. After they had their shopping done, my father would send them up to the kitchen, which was our living room. It was taken for granted that my mother would feed them well for the journey back home, across the silver strand that stretched from our house to almost the bottom of Point.

Point was also called Carrickfinn, which means Fair Rock in Irish. The old name for the peninsula is Ros Scaite which means Flung (or Scattered) Headland. The German philosopher, Martin Heidegger, might have felt at home here because of the existential character of the name. This is the way he views the nature of our existence: *geworfen - flung, scattered* or *dropped* – literally the way a dog drops a litter of pups. It is wonderful to think that there were existentialists in Donegal in the old days, giving names to our far-flung headlands. Theoretically, with names like that, we should have been in a state of pure nature - and who knows, maybe we were. In any case, we were well west of Eden!

Carrickfinn now has a modern airport and the runway is straight up and down the neck of the sandy banks, which connect the mainland with the peninsula. At one time, even in my memory, the waters of the Atlantic used to connect with the waters of its own tide - at the narrowest part of its neck - through a channel that filled up with the incoming tide. But in the intervening years, the ocean threw up enough sand to make the neck of the peninsula wider and stronger and there is no longer a connection between the tides.

There was a cart track that went back before living memory and the carts had a point where they could ford the channel. In time, the cart track gave way to a tarred road that could carry cars and small lorries. Then came a tarred road, and several years ago Carrickfinn Airport was built. It changed the place utterly and forever.

Railroad stations, trains in the night,
Greyhound buses, flashing lights,
Someone's leavin', someone's left behind
It's the same old story time after time...
Someone is always sayin' goodbye

My mother came to the airport last Christmas to see me off on my return trip to Boston over Dublin. She had never come before despite many coaxings, but this time there was no need to persuade her. She just asked for her shoes, a sign that she was coming with us. She was wearing the mauve dress she liked so much with her black overcoat.

The lobby of the airport was cold, so my niece Marion put her black throw-shawl around my mother to keep her warm. The place was not too crowded and we found a quiet corner by the window to chat for a few minutes, and where she could sit and watch the plane take off.

We said our goodbyes, with promises to call. As I got ready to go through the gate, the children ran down along the cyclone fence around the runway, so that they could be the last to wave goodbye. The plane taxied in a circle before take-off, and I could see from my window seat my mother's tiny figure with the shawl around her head. She looked so pale and small in the distance.

The image of the distant face shrouded in black would stay with me on the journey. I did not think I would ever see her again, she had become so tiny and frail. I wept softly as the plane began its smooth lift off to the east, because I knew she would watch until it was lost in the clouds. She would then go home, with a heart that was sad and heavy - but one that was already hopeful of the next return. She would light the holy candle and pray until I had come safely home to Stonehill. When I called to say I was safely back, the candle would be extinguished.

Coming safely home - that was a big thing for her and could be easily described as the metaphor by which she viewed our *existing,* our *Dasein,* as Heidegger would put it. That daunting philosophical word - in German - only means *our being there,* or the *way we exist in this world.* We were all included in this, three generations of us. While any one of us was in peril of the journey, Maggie became the restless one who prayed for our guidance.

I never thought she regarded *the travel itself* as perilous - she saw that just as part of life that was woven into our destiny - but rather what could befall us on life's way. *Life's way is not always our way,* and I think it was here that she made the distinction. One need not come safely home from life's way. Indeed, one need not come home again – ever.

There was always a special prayer for those who were *most at risk.* That could be our father, any one of her seven children, their spouses, or any of the grandchildren, or their offspring. I think there was another list that included dad's folk, her own folk, and whoever else got caught up into her compassion - tramps or drunks, elderly women living alone, wayward young ones, or those who got left straggling behind wherever we were going. Even in the countryside, where people are kinder, there were always those who got left behind.

In the early 40s, Maggie had begun to send money to the *Massachusetts Home for Little Wanderers.* Hardly anyone in our area would have known of such a place, because we barely knew where America was. But the name - wherever she came across it - would have appealed to her, gone straight to her heart, and on to her giving list. Strangely enough, the *Home for Little Wanderers* still exists in Boston, but I remember being enchanted by the name - printed on the envelopes which arrived at our house - because it sounded like a place where I could meet Mickey Rooney or Spencer Tracy. However, I doubt its clientele is as *innocent* now as it was in the early years of the war.

As Maggie grew older I celebrated Mass in my grandfather's house each evening for herself, her sister Sarah and other family members - when I was home on vacation, or on a short visit between business trips. There was a room there, nicely appointed, and rarely used. It was a perfect place to steal away around five or six o'clock in the evening. We bothered no one, but word would go around the houses and, consequently, there was usually a small group of adults and children who attended each day.

There is a time in the order of the Mass where silence is observed, usually after the reception of the Eucharist. Ours was never overly long because the children were always poised to try to make each other laugh, by making faces or *acting the maggot.*

Sometimes during this silent time, the name of one or another of her children or grandchildren would emerge audibly from my mother's whispered prayer, and one could guess of whom she was thinking and why. She herself was not aware of this. It was just that the intensity of her prayer broke though the surface of the meditation period we were observing.

In the last years, it was mostly the grandchildren who were in the forefront of her consciousness and, therefore, her prayer - those who were alone, or hurting, confused about their way forward in life, or trapped in their compulsions. Maggie was also keenly aware of the *contagion of nameless evil* that could befall any of us, and was anxious that we might find our way out of the suffering that might entail.

She never knew, as parents often do not know, the risks we ran in our individual lives. We oftentimes spared her the details of what we thought might distress her, and she never pressed us about the negative moments in each other's lives. She just intuited far more than we ever knew.

Will ye no' come back again?
Will ye no' come back again?
Better lo'ed ye canna' be,
Will ye no' come back again...

My mother lived a simple and uncomplicated life. That comes naturally to no one, and I don't think it came naturally to her either. But *it seemed* to come naturally to her. It seemed like *a given* in her life. When my brother Hugh said about her, *"Bhí sí nádúrtha* – she was natured", it was the highest compliment that can be bestowed on anyone in the ancient Gaelic language. Yet, Maggie had to work at being human like everyone else who wants to improve their lives in an ethical way or, similarly, like anyone who wants to deepen, not only their faith, but also their *union* with the God they hope to see someday.

Therein lay her secret. To say where the *natural self* left off and the *graced* self took on - was impossible. To the observer, and even to her children, her actions looked seamless and fully human. Even her faults and limitations were human too. Of course, how could they not be? Creatures born into a bent world cannot escape flaws in their character, either from nature or from nurture. The struggle to be human is one that is laid on all of us, and some carry more baggage than others.

Grace builds upon nature, or makes nature *more natural* or *gracious*. The theology of all this is sometimes too much for me. I think of it as being like the little eddies on the face of flowing water. They look just like dimples, but they go deep. I cannot go as deep as the source of my mother's life - and I was not her confessor or spiritual guide. But her ordinary life hinted that it had another - deeper - component. I think I can recall some of those hints, which I have called *'Habits of a Mother's Heart'*.

*   *   *   *

17

A short time after our Christmas farewell, Maggie caught a 'flu that was going around. Then her lungs became infected and she developed congestive heart failure. Despite a good Christmas and New Year, her health had taken a spiral downwards that none of us would have predicted, and faster than any of us thought possible.

I heard of her condition while at Stonehill College in Massachusetts, where I live and work and it was as if my premonitions about our recent parting were coming true. But I had determined that I would not return home again until I heard of her death. I marshaled my reasons: I did not want to go through the emotion of another final farewell - it was too wrenching. Besides, I was frequently in touch with her by telephone, sometimes talking to her, sometimes just leaving a message of love and good wishes.

Then there was the other thing I dreaded: arriving at home in a tired and emotional condition. If I waited until she died - I had told myself - at least I would be able to have a good, quiet cry on my own. Then get on with the serious work of preparing her funeral liturgy, making the journey, greeting the people at the wake and celebrating her funeral. It was all very tidy in my mind and in synch with my controlling nature.

Of course, I knew there would be pressure to change those plans, so in the conversations that took place over the ensuing weeks, I took the time to make my position clear to my brothers Hugh and John. They understood my reasons and it was not a problem for them. In any case, John was as cognizant as I was about the need to make timely preparations. He would be in charge of digging her grave and filling it in again, probably with the help of the older grandchildren, his own son Jim, Owen and Seán McFadden, and Tom McDonald. None of us, however, suspected how far ahead the final parting would be.

Around mid-March when things were looking particularly bad for my mother, my sister-in-law Kathleen undertook the charge to make me change my mind. She couched her initial request in the news that Claire, her daughter, was on her way home from California. Claire was the only one of the grandchildren who had not seen Maggie for quite a while, and Claire was hoping that her granny would keep death at bay *for her* until she arrived home.

Kathleen, who has oftentimes been persuasive, and always very helpful to me, said she thought that I also should come home. She added that despite the fact of Maggie's being very low, the situation in the house was not what I imagined it to be. It was not sad or gloomy, but on the contrary, each one seemed to be drawing strength from the others. She thought I should share the experience.

This was just two weeks before Easter. When I looked at the calendar and saw that, because of Holy Week, there were going to be some down days at the College, I decided to go. Anyway, I had to celebrate the Paschal Mystery somewhere, so why not spend this last Passover of my mother with the family? I also noted that even if I got there before my mother died, the wake and funeral would probably be over by Easter.

I had some preparations to make for the journey, so I made them and went back to Donegal.

Home is the Hunter

See yon London lights are burning
Thru' the frost and weary snow;
Sleep on, sleep on, my little darling,
Because your Daddy's comin' home...

What happened in the next two weeks was an eye-opener for me and for many others in the household. It revealed a side of my mother, which I had neither known of before, nor even dreamt of its existence. It also caused an aspect of my *own persona* to become bare to my close scrutiny. It was an aspect that I found humiliating.

March was a relatively mild month in Ireland that year, although now and then there came a strong hail shower to remind us that we had just inched away from winter. Maggie had a good, quiet sleep before I arrived, so she actually looked fresher than I felt after a transatlantic journey. When I mentioned how well she looked my sister-in-law Sheila and niece Margaret Mary agreed that morning freshness was one of the constants in her demeanor. But they also pointed out that it could change as rapidly as the March weather.

Maggie seemed to have limited breathing capacity in her lungs, but used it economically to greet people and say a few words. Sometimes she leaned forward while in a sitting position. This position was the only one that gave her comfort; the others seem to leave her prey to the relentless rise of the fluid in her lungs. At other times she would fall asleep in this leaning-forward mode, and gradually yield to a heavy torpor. Then her face would change dramatically. The blood in her cheeks would gather in little clusters, and a ghastly purplish pallor settle around her mouth and nose. *It was Death preparing Its face in her body.*

*   *   *   *

I could not resist asking why I was home again, despite my own counter intention. Kathleen was the one who called and made the gentle persuasion. When I asked her if the idea had originated with herself, she admitted that my sister Margaret had a great deal to do with it.

Margaret, in turn, said that, yes, she was very much behind the idea, but quickly added that the rest of the family was too. They had talked, and felt that I should be there for my own good. They felt badly that I was on my own, relying on phone calls for information, and always waiting for the call that would come out of the blue. They also knew that I was missing out on the dynamism of strength, which they felt like a magnetic field around all of them. Margaret also said she was afraid that if I were not there, I might have misgivings later about my absence.

I was deeply touched by these conversations, and through them, I felt as if my being were raised to another level. What they were telling me, in effect, was that they had a community of caring which was functioning at a high level, and that they wanted me to belong to it. Indeed, although they did not say this, as long as I stayed apart from it, they would have regarded me as impoverished.

It did not take me long to realize that the spirit which Kathleen had tried to describe to me was, indeed, a reality. There was a great deal of happiness in our home, and people were drawing strength from each other. The source of the strength was not a mystery.

The mystery resides precisely in what Robert Lipsyte recently wrote about his own dying wife in *The Country of Illness:*

> "There was great love in that room, and it was emanating from her, and flowing through us, and gave us strength to overcome our own fears, our own weaknesses, and stay, and be with her."

I felt a need to send an e-mail message back to Stonehill every so often, simply to keep them aware of what was happening. After all, I had left for what I thought would be a wake and funeral. Given the greatly weakened state of my mother when I arrived, I expected her time with us would be a countdown - and so I began to number the days. There was no doubt in my mind; I expected the time to be short.

*   *   *   *

March 17

> Hail, glorious, Saint Patrick, dear saint of our isle,
> On us, thy dear children, bestow a sweet smile;
> O thou, who art high in thy mansions above,
> On Erin's green valleys, look down in thy love.

The day I arrived in Calhame was St. Patrick's Day, but I guess I did not notice it much or forgot quickly. Usually I am both in Washington, DC, and New York City on this day, playing my accustomed exhibitionist role in the festivities that surround St. Patrick's celebration in the United States.

My niece Claire had arrived home from northern California earlier in the day - actually in the wee hours of the morning. Much to her relief, she found her granny not only alert, but waiting very hard for her. Some cell-phone calls on the progress of her journey by car from Dublin allowed those at home to relay the news to Maggie.

All observers agree on one fact: had my mother not been alert, Claire's arrival would not have registered with her at all. Claire, for her part, knew as she made her journey that my mother was low that day. But those at home said Claire never knew how low. They expected the next short coma to be the end.

Their reunion was emotional, and it sparked in Maggie a *will-to-being* that Viktor Frankl would have used as an example to stress his central theme: that *Meaning* (or *Logos*) is the central thrust in human life. Indeed, the reunion with Claire was so intense that it could have wiped out whatever strength Maggie had left.

Yet, for two hours, the two of them had time only for each other, my mother running her hand through the rich mane of Claire's red hair, fondling her cheeks, and telling her how wonderful it was to see her again. Claire has a bubbly, cheerful personality and she expresses her feelings easily. She was reciprocating Maggie's emotion, so much so, that her mother Kathleen finally had to tell her to calm down, for fear that she would take my mother overboard with emotions of joy and love.

When we were children, we often used to call our former home, *The Hive*, because of the constant flow of visitors to the house and to the shop. But it never was such a hive of activity as this one to which I had come home. The besieged hub of the comings and the goings was my mother's bedroom, especially on the part of the grandchildren, Danny and the twins, Bartley and Mairéad, who took turns sitting with her. Great-grandchildren Kevin, Sarah, and Conor McDonald were also part of this band of little watchers.

The *Dubliners* - who were comprised of Tadhg and his family, Hugh's girls, and Kathleen's children - had all come down at the weekend in anticipation of their Granny's death, but they had to leave the following day to return to school, or to work. They did so with great reluctance because they had been prepared to stay the course with Maggie. My brother Tadhg also left reluctantly, postponing departure to his own school in Dublin until five o' clock on Monday morning. Since the journey could not be tailored to the minute on a weekday morning, headmaster Tadhg MacPháidín would be late for school that day.

March 18

Even though Dr. Bonar, the physician who sees her most - along with Nurse Geraldine, both of whom are most attentive to her, and kind - says she is slipping away and there is nothing more he can do, it is still hard to say when she will die. Her face and body are well nourished, but the steady rise of the fluid in her lungs makes even a partial recovery doubtful. Maggie's three nieces, Mary Bheag, Brigid and Fia, came from the Foreland today. She was glad to see them, and they lit a special spark in her, as she ever had great fondness for them.

The tide that flows through the Calhame Bridge, below our window, is flooding as I write these words. The daffodils are to be seen everywhere in the fields. Up in the hills, the ewes are lambing, and new life is all about. The temperature is a mild 50°F, almost summer in these high latitudes.

Breakfast is ready, and the smell of frying bacon and fresh sausage is too good to ignore. Another day is beginning, and it will be devoted to the care of one person on the part of many, and of the many more that stand behind them waiting for a call.

The many will give of themselves to the care of the one, and they will not stint or grow tired. There is an overabundance in their hearts to do more than they actually achieve. So they will fluff the pillows a little extra, pull them this way or that, shade the blinds the right way, or clasp Maggie's hands resting on the lacy-white bedspread in front of her. Maggie reminds me of Penelope awaiting the return of Ulysses, in Wallace Stevens' poem, *The World as Meditation*:

"The barbarous strength within her would never fail...
She would talk a little to herself as she combed her hair,
Repeating his name with its patient syllables,
Never forgetting him that kept constantly coming so near."

A thought went up my mind that I should be glad to die in the midst of such love. But since I am neither dying, nor likely to be ushered so gently *"into that good night"*, I can profit from a more mundane pleasure: the joy of having breakfast at home, where there is such an air of well being and peace.

I was struck with a singular emotion this morning and suspect it was one that took its time percolating slowly through the layers of dense, and sometimes reified, emotions that have been laid down relentlessly over the years. It can be stated simply: it was just that *I was home again* in a way I had not been since childhood.

My goings had started by transferring to Dore School when I was ten. That was young enough for someone even as precocious and as adventurous as I was. Others would substitute *'pure spoiled brat'* for that latter description - but whatever the valid reading of the character that went away, there was probably a part of me that was missing until I discovered it again.

*   *   *   *

Home is the hunter,
Home from the hill;
And the sailor, home
From the sea...

Home is a word that people toss around with great frequency, but we have to remind ourselves that it is a polyvalent word. It has to carry many layers of meaning, the baggage of centuries, of cultures alien and near, from every mother's son who ever walked through the doorway and said, *'I'm home'*, to every father's daughter who slippered across a threshold to make her home in another's house.

Home is made up of all the meanings we have lived through, many more that we haven't lived through - and others that appear in the whiny periods of late adolescence or young adulthood. Thus, we may conclude that we missed out on something, or were deprived of what the others got. Like it or not, we will always have people who will raise whining to a high art because they turn narcissistic and can never escape from the condition.

Home is a combination of love and reaction, of pre-conscious sentiments, of filled and unfulfilled psychic needs, physical needs, everything from a warm bed to what Robert Frost describes as:

> "the place where, when you have to go there,
> They have to take you in."

It is not given easily to any man or woman to describe this reality called home. Might as well describe the way the tops of the trees meet the sky, or the manner in which waves break, before and after they hit the strand. Different each time, but the sky or the shore - like the inborn dream of home - *are never violated.*

The truth, I now realize, is that I was called home so that a birth could take place in those parts of me that were barren . . . atrophied . . . truncated. The words of TS Eliot in *The Journey of the Magi* came to mind:

> "Were we led all that way for?
> Birth or death? ....I had seen birth and death.
> And thought they were different..."

That *a birth* did take place I now know, and I can't exactly say from where to what. But my mind changed, and so did my heart. I am working on the unruly emotions, and wondering like Goethe, if they were ever baptized.

But, I have something new to say now. And this is happening towards the end of a busy and professional life, from which my priesthood was not excluded. Rather, it was marginalised due to the onus of every college and university president to build facilities; to do public relations, to lobby Washington and Boston to fund student scholarships. Also, to attend to relations within the university with faculty, administration and students; to tend to the relationships outside the university, with alumni, with parents, with trustees and benefactors – and the general public.

Yes, I experienced new life during those few weeks I spent at home. But I never expected it to happen in the abode of death...

*   *   *   *

March 20

Claire became the number one night-person at her own request. Last night she woke me around three or four in the morning with her loud praying. I never heard Claire pray before, and I was sure that Maggie was dying, so I rushed into her room, which was adjacent to mine. Claire said no, there was nothing wrong, and mother was only having a restless night. Praying was her way of trying to get Maggie back to sleep. I stayed with them for a little while to assure myself that it was just restlessness; then I returned to my own sleep, which in Donegal - some say because of the ozone that rises off the ocean - always comes so quickly and so easily.

The doctor increased Maggie's diuretic pill to 1.5 mg today. That means she has to be lifted out of bed more often. The diuretic weakens her and so does the handling, even though it is ever so gentle. She says she is weary but not in pain. She can still smile and make jokes. Tadhg said in a phone call this afternoon that she is not yet quite ready to write the end to the script.

It was another beautiful day, and I went walking on the White Strand this evening. The ocean was absolutely blue from shore to horizon, with the islands strung low across the sky like a necklace: Owey, The Stags, Inisfree, and Gola. There was freshness in the wind, and a hundred tiny perfumes, as it blew over the dunes and the seagrass - which the local people call *bent*. Already the yellow fleabanes and cream primroses were in flower, tucked modestly into the sides of the sea-banks along the water. Here and there, a single blue bell was inviting the whole world to dance.

Today is the vernal equinox, and from now on the days will be getting longer until the summer solstice. Then it will be so lightsome in Donegal, that visitors will be fooled by the lateness of the hour. We are not too near the Arctic Circle, so we do not have anything as spectacular as the *white nights of St. Petersburg*, but we are on the 56th parallel, which is as far north as Labrador in Canada. On these particular evenings of the vernal equinox, the Hale-Bopp comet can be seen blazing brightly in the evening sky.

My nieces, Marion and Claire, are doing the nightshift with Maggie tonight. Then Sheila, Margaret Mary and Martha will take over during the day. When Hugh's younger daughters take their turn, my brother Jim, home from London, refers to them as *The Spice Girls*. Jim always makes sure the turf fire is blazing brightly. Brother Hugh is always on call, night or day. Paddy will stop by sometime during the afternoon, and spread-eagle himself on the edge of the bed, his legs on a chair and his head next to his mother's - on her pillow. John will come in the late evening hours after his work to hear the news of the day, and to revise estimates for the timing for the digging of Maggie's grave.

And my sister Margaret – whom we all call *Martha* now - is busy keeping the house running, and keeping an eye on all that is going on, making tea and apple tart for those who come by to see what is happening. This is Donegal where no one hesitates to call or come visit. With the telephone going all day, it makes for a very busy house. I try to be helpful with the visitors, but mostly I try to be – just be – and pray with my mother, and the family.

* * * *

March 22

It is a stormy day. *Maggie is much the same, although now she says she wants to get better and so she must start* praying *to do so.* We do not take this seriously, and even if she is serious - the doctor said yesterday that her pulse was stronger - it will be a hard fight.

The caravan of Dubliners arrived last night: Mary de Lourdes, Nora and Sinéad are Hugh and Sheila's girls. Niamh, Daire and Colm are Tadhg and Eithne's children. Marion, Danny and the twins are four of John and Kathleen's six. Some of them are already on their Easter holidays and some must go back tomorrow, to work until Wednesday, and then return again. Young Jim is in the Jersey Islands at his work. In any case, it means that Maggie will not want for eager carers this week.

March 25

Mother is propped upon her pillows, dressed in a lovely pink nightdress. Margaret Mary just did her hair, pulled back naturally, the way she likes it. She has fallen asleep again, her high cheekbones more evident now in her illness.

When I went in this morning to give her a kiss that my cousins, Bella and Pat in Yonkers, asked me to give her, I was wearing a new pair of striped pyjamas. She looked at me from head to toe, and I said *"How do you like my new pyjamas"?* She nodded approvingly and wanted to know if they were Japanese. I said yes, but the label might have said otherwise.

The doctor is with her now, and says he finds her better. Since he said yesterday - and two days ago - that it was all over, and the only thing that mattered was to keep her comfortable, my sister instinctively pushed me after him to press him for more information.

Having been pushed almost into his back, I know my face broke into an involuntary smile when he turned around and I asked the question. He said she was stable, and told me he had given her until the weekend, last week. Now he does not know. He asked me how long I was staying.

In the evening of this day, the Feast of the Annunciation, a good friend of our family and a favourite of my mother, Fr. Eugene Greene, arrived for a visit. It was after the evening Mass that I had celebrated in her room. Everyone had left the room, and I was hanging up my stole or doing something similar. mother was lying on her left side facing the window. Fr. Eugene went around to that side, sat on the edge of her bed, and began to talk to her.

I dropped to my knees for no particular reason. Having just celebrated Mass, I did not intend to pray, and since I was on the other side of the bed, mother was not aware of my presence - or at least I thought not. Afterwards, she asked someone who the other *"older gentleman"* in the room was, but she may have seen me leave the room, which was partially darkened anyway. Thus, I was able to rationalize her unflattering remark.

It started off simply enough. Fr. Eugene asked her in Irish,

"*An bfhuil pían ar bith ort?* - Is there any pain on you?
"*Níl, ach tá eagla orm!* - No! But there is fear on me".
"*Cé'n t-eagla 'tá ort?* – He asked softly- What fear is on you"?
"*Nach bfuíghidh mé biseach.* - That I will not get better. "

Those were the words that were spoken. I was the witness in the shadows. My ears were perked. Two questions were asked and two questions were answered. Then came the event.

At that moment mother raised herself from her semiprone position on her left side, and sat up straight in the bed. And for the next fifteen to twenty minutes, she prayed, as I had never heard anyone pray before. But it was not the prayer of the dying - *Into Your Hands, O Lord, I commend my spirit* - that she prayed. It was the prayer of someone who wanted to get better. It was a bold, pleading, yet insistent prayer: *Sacred Heart of Jesus, make me better...*

The first thing I want to say with conviction is this: it was my mother's voice that was praying - *and it was not*. The sheer volume of her voice was not something of which she was capable. There was a part of the praying voice that was male, *a basso profondo*, and it mingled with her own voice in a way that was almost polyphonic. But at the higher reaches it was perceptibly my mother's voice.

The second thing I want to say with humiliation is that her prayer threw me into utter confusion, because my faith was not strong enough to affirm her prayer. Inside my head, I was thinking, *"Dearest mother, you are on the edge of death, and it would be so much easier for us, and happier for you, if you prayed for your happy death".*

Like a good soldier, Eugene stuck to his post, but after fifteen minutes or so, he was overcome with tears and had to leave the room. I remained kneeling at the other side of the bed, with my head buried in my hands. I was in mental turmoil because I wanted the right thing for her, and I thought she was asking for the wrong thing. There was another thing that humiliated me: in this one situation where I should have been a strength to her, I was a wretched weakling. I had reached a limitation of my own faith, I had crossed the border of cowardice, and I did not like it. I did not like myself either.

Shortly afterwards, I left the room quietly, hoping that I would not be noticed by my mother or by anyone else. Later, I asked Eugene what he thought of what we had witnessed. He said he never heard anything like it in his lifetime.

Neither had I - even though I had been to many meetings of charismatic Christians, and had heard people praying in tongues, none of them ever struck me as authentic. It always seemed as if those praying knew a smattering of Hebrew words. I always remained impervious to these manifestations of the Spirit, but it occurred to me often that if I started praying *as Gaeilge*, I could sound every bit as mystifying.

But the praying of Maggie was different. It was *strong, bold, insistent and pleading*. It went beyond her strength and her condition. It was also very understandable. This loud praying was to happen several times again in the following days with several others startled by the same phenomenon. There was no doubt in my mind that Maggie was praying as if she were possessed by another spirit.

*   *   *   *

Wednesday, March 26

On the heels of last night's experience, Wallace Stevens came swirling into my head:

> For she was the maker of the song she sang
> The ever-hooded, tragic-gestured sea
> Was merely a place by which she walked to sing.
> Whose spirit is this? We said, because we knew
> It was the spirit that we sought and knew
> That we should ask this often as she sang.

Yesterday I booked my flight for Monday, Dublin to Boston. That means I will have to leave Donegal on Easter Sunday shortly after noontime, and have a one night layover in Dublin.

Maggie had a fairly hyper kind of day yesterday, lots of visitors and no sleep. Toward evening, the idea that she would not sleep became a neuralgic point with her. My teetotaling siblings decided she should have a shot of brandy in her milk. Maggie never liked alcohol because she had seen too much of the evil it spawned, especially in families. I suspect if she had known the brandy was in the milk, she would have refused it.

I suggested a more ingenious and advanced solution - one of my sleeping pills - but they were afraid that the pill would knock her out forever. I argued for its relative mildness, since it took two of them to overcome my insomnia at night. But my pharmacological advice fell on deaf ears, and Maggie got the Borgia treatment, milk with something stronger in it.

Three cheers for the brandy! It did make her sleep and she looks very bright today. The nurse was in to check her and said she is the best she has seen her in a long time. The doctor prescribed a diuretic yesterday that does not deplete her potassium. He did not bother to do it last week, he told us, because he expected her to die at the end of the week before last.

My sister Margaret and I took a walk by the shore yesterday. My mind was still roiled by the lines of Stevens, *"Whose spirit is this? We said because we knew / it was the spirit that we sought / and knew that we should ask this often when she ... sang..."*

The sea was high because it was the time of the *"rabharta"* or spring tide. The wind was high too, and it chased the foam from the surf across the sand, changing its pure white froth to a lacy-beige organza that died in its own bubbles as it stranded itself on the brownish sand.

We saw a dead seal being rolled in by the waves, beached, and then taken out on the next wave. Its head was gruesomely bashed in. We stopped to look.

A closer look revealed that the seal's head had been eaten off, and the sight of it was too much for my sister to bear. She was painfully dealing with her mother's dying and anything that touched on death was too raw for her nerves.

We walked on – with the wind beating the sand into our faces and blowing us sideways at times. In many ways, we had never been together on a farther and wilder shore than this – and it was important that we walk together.

Days of Passion

"When the time came, he took his place at table . . . and he said to them, 'I have ardently longed to eat this Passover with you, before I suffer'."   Lk. 22:14

Holy Thursday, March 27

There was a storm out at sea yesterday and we are getting the spin-off in the form of dreary, cold weather. Maggie is not at her best today. Her pulse is all right, but there is a slight aspiration in her throat, which the nurse thinks may be heart-related. Last night, Maggie suddenly took to speaking in Irish, even when she was being spoken to in English. She has her arms held more tightly against her body. Everyone has their own theories, but I think she is going backwards every day.

It is Easter weekend, and her grandchildren Owen and Seán, with their spouses and children, will be home from London and Leeds respectively. My brother Tadhg will arrive sometime today. His son Daire has already been here, and left to buy a car in Belfast. Niamh and Paddy and their children, Aoife and Ryan, will come on Saturday. Maggie likes to see the children and they have great affection for her. They also seem to understand what is happening.

It will be interesting to see how the children remember *this time*. The late writer from Georgia, Flannery O'Connor, remarks in her story, *The Artificial Nigger*, that the understanding of certain realities, like the *action of mercy*, is given in strange ways to children. Perhaps they understand more than we think they do - things from which we try to shield them, or that we explain away in an evasive or reductionist manner, as they begin to ask the questions for which we have no answers. Or maybe the questions we ourselves once asked but do so no longer....

We have a sizable crowd in the house for Mass every evening around five o'clock. Peggy Dunleavy comes every day with her son Danny. They recently lost Ambrose, Peggy's husband, to cancer of the throat, and Peggy is sorely grieved by the loss. So is Danny, but he can't show it as much. It is very interesting to see the special regard my mother has for Peggy because of her grief and loss, and it is touching how she reaches out to comfort Peggy, even though my mother is - by far - the more infirm.

Reaching out to comfort others came naturally to my mother, and it is delightful to see this habit still with her, even though she is debilitated enough by her own condition to become understandably narcissistic. All her life, she had a simple gesture of her head, hands, and especially of her eyes that indicated her compassion for others, especially when she was face to face with their grief.

Her eyes had a special way of showing that she was going out of herself towards the other person. There was no mistaking the warmth or the authenticity of her feeling. Along with her contagious kindness and joy, it was one of the gestures that replicated her whole being.

She welcomed people into her heart and home, and she was very tactile in expressing this welcome. She would take people by the hand, or by the arm, to show them the warmth of her heart. If she were sitting close to you, she might put her hand on your knee. The physical gesture and contact came naturally to her. Her need to touch also carried a strong element of trust, and seemed necessary for the full expression she needed to make. There was a total lack of rehearsal in her mode of action and no inhibition about the physical. Neither was she demonstrative about her touch. Indeed, she was probably unaware of it herself.

* * * *

"Then he withdrew from them, about a stone's throw away, and knelt down and prayed, 'Father', he said, 'if you are willing, take this cup away from me. Nevertheless, let your will be done not mine'. ...In his anguish, he prayed even more earnestly, and his sweat fell to the ground like great drops of blood."   Lk. 22; 41 ff.

Because of my experience with mother's prayer-in-the Spirit the other night, it became clear to me that this was *her agony* in the true sense. Many people refer to a person's agony when they are already in the throes of dying. This happens when the physical body begins to pit the unconscious will to live against the power of death. It is usually a short time before expiration.

I believe the *agony* comes earlier, that it is the intense spiritual struggle of the person with the fact that he or she must die. The word *agony* is taken from the Greek word *agōn,* which means contest or struggle. The agōn is what the gladiators did in the ring, but here it is between the dying person and a *fatum* – that which will be (literally, that which is *"spoken")*. Something like the *fatwa,* or the death-dealing sentence that the late Ayatollah Khomeini spoke upon Salman Rushdie for his alleged blasphemy against Islam.

For the believer, the agony can be understood as a struggle with the *fatum* of a personal God. Those who do not believe in a personal God must struggle against the *fatum* too. Here it can be called *fate,* in our modern understanding of the word, because it is a force that is at once *determinist* and *impersonal*. However, from an empirical point of view, it seems to me that the *sentence* or the *fatum* is the same reality for both believer and unbeliever, and the only thing that distinguishes the two is *what lies behind the fatum* – a personal God (Being) or impersonal fate (Whatever).

Another way to say this is that the *fatum* is the same for both believer and unbeliever. They are both objects of the *fatum,* because it is their death that is *spoken* in each instance, the *fatwa* is the same. The subject speaking the fatum is personal in one situation and impersonal in the other. *It seems to me Either/Or.* There is no *tertium quid.* There is not a third option.

I will not say that the struggle is easier for the believer than it is for the non-believer. Each one dies one's own death, each one's death is different – absent sudden death - and no one knows what one's reaction will be in the face of destiny or *"The Abyss",* as Aaron-Marie Cardinal Lustiger of Paris recently put it (and had to explain later to the ever-watchful press that he did not intend a *nihilist* connotation). We can hazard a good guess that our response will be emotional and - for certain - it will involve emotions of which we are unaware in the mundane affairs of everyday existence.

Anyone who would like a short dress-rehearsal would do well to read the magnificent little story by Leo Tolstoy called *The Death of Ivan Illich,* or consult the well-documented book by Elizabeth Kübler-Ross, *On Death and Dying,* wherein she analyses the different stages a person passes through on the way to death.

*   *   *   *

On Holy Thursday evening when we had the Liturgy of the Lord's Supper, I tried to indicate to the children and to the family that this was the time of Maggie's *passion*. She herself was paying close attention to what was being said, as she always did when it came to matters of worship. So my direct reference was not to her agony, but to the Agony of Christ in Gethsemane after the celebration of the Passover Supper.

He brought three of his disciples with him, and left them while he went a little farther. Knowing that betrayal and death lay before him, he nevertheless pleaded with his Father that this *"chalice"* might pass from him.

St. Luke, said to be a physician, reports in his account of the Passion that during this time of pleading, the sweat of Jesus fell to the ground *like great drops of blood*. Luke is also the writer who comments on the *'whiteness'* of Jesus during the Transfiguration, so his details are not to be ignored.

Historians generally do not have any difficulty with this passage because there is a phenomenon known as *hematidrosis,* and it is caused by the passing of hemoglobin - the coloured matter in blood - into the sweat glands. It is a sign, even though a rare one, of extreme anxiety. *But from the text it seems clear that the prospect of death, even in Jesus, precipitated a contest of wills, which may have been more painful than his subsequent crucifixion and death.*

I am not sure all the children understood what I was saying, but some of the older ones surely did. If not, they will understand it some day when they are in the ring of their personal *'agōn'* - or contest - which will surely come their way.

*   *   *   *

I will buy my love a shroud of the ornamental brown;
And while they are a-making it the tears,
They will flow down;
For once I had a true love but now he's dead and gone,
but the Bonny Boy is young and he's growing....

March 28, Good Friday

It is Good Friday, and the faithful are in the village chapel, *Saint Mary - Star of the Sea*, as I write this. Good Friday was always the most momentous day of my childhood years.

It was a common feature of the pre-Conciliar Church that it placed more emphasis on the passion and death of Christ than it did on the Resurrection. This was true of pre-Vatican II in Ireland as well. Perhaps it is not fair to generalise too much, since the faithful themselves determine the nature of their devotion, and it could well be that it was our received culture, especially the inherited memories of the Great Hunger, that predisposed us to pick out those moments of salvation history that have to do with suffering.

Others would maintain that the Irish character itself vacillates between asceticism and hedonism, and my childhood years could have been part of the natural swing between those extremes. Another observer of the Irish soul describes us as being in a metaphysical suspension between this world and the next, and never at home in either. This would indicate some kind of blessed rage, perhaps for *absolute* - perhaps for *order,* or for *oblivion.*

Whatever the case, Good Friday was always a day of mourning - intensely so. We never did anything, and often never even spoke, before three o'clock in the afternoon, which the Scriptures relate as the hour of Christ's death on the Cross.

The natural world of the westerly parts of Ireland conspired in our mourning. When the phenomena that accompanied the death of Jesus were proclaimed in the Scriptures, it was not hard for a child to see them repeated in the Irish sky.

Often, we read the face of nature to see if our own grief were somehow mirrored there. *"Sunt lacrimae rerum - there are tears of* things" – the words from Virgil's *Aeneid* always seem to describe the souls of children when they try to grasp something of the divine tragedy of our faith. If it happened once, a child thinks, it can happen again. Thus, it would not surprise us if darkness again covered the earth on Good Friday.

*   *   *   *

But today is bright and springlike, with a refreshing breeze, *and I no longer have a childlike outlook on the world or on the Lord's passion.* I have learnt enough in my lifetime to be able to see the Lord's passion not only in the historical event, but equally so *in the agony of men and women, as part of the human - and the inhuman - condition.*

So much of what we call the human condition is suffering which we inflict on ourselves, on others, or they on us. There is enough of this to go around the world thousands of times over. And if the Lord is in solidarity with the poor and suffering, as Matthew 25 seems to suggest, then there seems to be enough inflicted pain *to ensure that the Lord will be in agony until the end of time.*

Our age had added a new dimension to the human condition, with its wars and gulags, its holocausts and ethnic cleansings. A new factor is added in our time, and it is the fate of the young, the unborn and the born.

It seems to me that there are no measuring scales vast enough to weigh the injustices against the *'potential'* humanity of the young. And there is hardly anything sadder than the fate many young people who never even get *a start* on their humanity, especially those who get a whiff of our world and want nothing more to do with it. For too many young people, addiction is almost a certainty, and suicide is often relief.

*   *   *   *

My mother's restlessness confirms for me that the turmoil comes from deep inside her. These past days have not been good; she has been in conflict between life and death, and there was another *"turn"* last night. We were all summoned to her bedside to pray, and Hugh again gave her a few spoonfuls of brandy with hot water and sugar. She calmed down after a while but did not sleep.

After we left, Sheila and Claire stayed with her. She wanted to pray, so they did. They prayed all night long. Sheila has long been accustomed to making the pilgrimage to Lough Derg, a place of penance dating back to medieval times. It is otherwise known as St. Patrick's Purgatory, and is located on an island in the middle of a lake in County Donegal, on the border with Northern Ireland.

The first exercise at Lough Derg is an all-night vigil. Part of the penance is that you pray, and since you have to stay awake, praying accomplishes that end as well as anything else. Sheila said this morning that she could not recall a night when she prayed more than last night. They prayed in Irish and in English, and they prayed every prayer and litany they could think of.

Maggie kept the pace, praying with them all the way, and knew all the words of the prayers they started. When they finally ran out of prayers, they stopped, fatigued by the spiritual effort of their vigil.

Saturday, March 29

As *Radio Telefís Éireann,* the national television station, is covering the Easter Vigil in Derrybeg Church tonight, I called the pastor, Fr. Michael Sweeney, to ask him if I might join him as concelebrant. He said a quick and enthusiastic yes, so I went off to join him.

My cousin Baba Brennan and her daughter and son, Máire and Pól Brennan of the singing group *Clannad,* were the stars of the choir. Máire was doing vocals and Pól the flute for a new Mass, composed by Liam Lawton. The parish choir had rehearsed endlessly for the event, and the Easter Vigil Liturgy was celebrated in the best traditions of the Donegal Gaeltacht and in the native tongue.

Before going to Mass, I went in to see my mother to tell her where I was going – and that I would pray for her in a special way during the celebration of the Paschal Mystery. She grasped my hand but said nothing. She was too weak to watch anything, so there was no point in bringing a television set into her bedroom. I was very conscious all during Mass that I would have to leave home again and go through another goodbye.

I was also feeling not a little guilty because I had brought with me a printed program from the College, in sufficient number, for her funeral Liturgy. The program had been put together by Kim Hess, our College organist, and Sheila Martin in Campus Ministry. When I first arrived home in Donegal on March 17th, I shoved the sizable cardboard box in which the programs were packed under my bed.

I told no one about the box, except my sister Margaret and I did so at the risk of upsetting her, because she could have seen the programs as a sign of hopelessness on my part. On the other hand, if I did not tell her, there was another risk of her putting the box in the attic. All of us, large and small, knew that whatever went into Margaret's attic need never appear again.

Sunday, March 30

> O we all went down to Mick McGilligan's ba...al
> Where they had to tear the paper off the wa...al
> To make room for all the people in the ha..al
> O the boys and the girls had the devil of a time
> At Mick McGilligan's Ball.

I was struck by the resemblance of Maggie's bedroom to the lines from the ballad, *Mick Mc Gilligan's Ball*. So many had gathered for the celebration of the Easter Liturgy, it seemed that even the wallpaper space was needed. It was a tight squeeze, with about seventeen of us, propped around the edges of the bed, sitting on the floor and wherever. We had a few chairs for guests but the rest had to make do.

I was squeezed into one corner of the room, seated on a chair, with a little table in front of me to serve as an altar. There was barely room for the chalice and the paten, two lit candles and a bloom of yellow roses someone had sent for Easter. If there was a faintly unceremonious air to the way we were spaced, there certainly was a strong feeling of community.

My mother was resting on the raised pillows, looking fresh and radiant in a colourful new nightgown. My mother was more comfortable and at home in worship than most people I have ever known. Being surrounded by people who were praying made her even more at home. It was extra special when all those in the room with her were those she loved.

When we were younger, John, Tadhg and myself used to pile on to the bed beside her, in the morning or at night, or whenever, maybe when she was taking a nap. I don't know when this started but I know I didn't make it up. So those who were older must have handed it down. Maggie used to pretend that the bed was *"The Derry Boat"* and we were all sailing away to Scotland on it. Now in her sickness-unto-death, this must have been *the ultimate Derry Boat for all of us,* because Maggie never had so many piled onto her bed as she had this day.

*   *   *   *

The Derry Boat was a well-known reality in Donegal. It sailed between Derry and Glasgow, and ferried countless emigrants from the northwest corner of Ireland to the Scottish work force, to field and fishing-port, to city and hamlet. If it had a glamorous sound of faraway places for children, places that ultimately would be bound up with their destiny, in reality it was a cattle boat owned by the Burns & Laird Company. It carried passengers above, cattle below.

A trip on *the Derry Boat* was really a wretched affair. The tea tasted like bilgewater, the sausages and rolls were thin and tasteless, and there was a pervasive smell of stale beer. The nadir of life was palpable, especially when the boat cleared Malin Head and hit the Sea of Moyle, and most everyone became so seasick that they did not care where they lay, or what they looked like.

Calm usually returned when the boat entered the mouth of the Clyde and steamed past all John Brown's shipyards until it came to anchor at the Broomie Law. By that time, people had freshened up a little and were passable looking, at least, for early morning arrival in Glasgow.

Despite its mundane reality and depressing destination, *the Derry Boat* was a rite of passage for young men or women. It was the way to a livelihood, and a means of supporting the families and the children who remained at home. Looking back on it now, I realize that while we were part of Ireland politically, we were an arm of the Scottish economy, and bound to Britain by ties deeper than we cared to acknowledge.

The Irish did the work, which the Scots and the English found unacceptable. Our own country provided a basic infrastructure of roads and schools and transportation. But it was Scotland, and the emigrant's sweat that put the bread on the Donegal table.

So *the Derry Boat* went down in history as ambivalent as it came up into it, a foul and stinking ship, and yet a symbol of independence and freedom with a certain hint of glory. Young people often conspired with each other to run away from home, knowing that some caring adult from their village would find them the price of passage, and put them on a bus to a kind landlady who would keep them while they looked for work.

The next Christmas home in Donegal, they would have coins to jingle in their pockets, and like *Pip* in Dickens', *Great Expectations,* when he returned from London, they would have *"a pint of condescension for all "*.

*   *   *   *

All around me hat I wear a tricoloured ribbon,
All around me hat, and it's a beauty to see
And if anybody asks me the reason why I wear it
I wear it for my true love whom I never more shall see.

On this Easter Sunday, Maggie was captain of the Derry Boat as she lovingly scanned every face on board, as if she were making a mental note of her shipmates and crew. Celebrating the Eucharist in this atmosphere was such a pleasure, such an easy thing to do - and to speak of new life and Resurrection seemed like comfortable old certitudes.

The faithful in the pews never realize how hard or how easy they can make the celebration of the Eucharist for a priest. I am often in situations where, as celebrant, I have to put all my psychic and spiritual energies into the creation of a faith-community of some semblance, even if it is only for a wedding or a funeral, where members of the congregation will never be together again.

I have been at some funerals where the liveliest body was the one in the coffin. It is impossible to do anything in a situation like that, except sweat it out. When you bend your knee, you wonder if you will ever be able to get up again - so strong is the downdrag.

At other times, when faith is a given, and a sense of community strong, I feel as if I am floating on a sea of serenity and the presence of God is palpable.

We sang "Happy Birthday" to Paddy before Mass. The windows were open and joy streamed out of that little room. It was carried all around the world with all the joy from other hearts that sensed the glory of the Resurrection. It will always remain a fresh, green garland of memory for all of us who were there.

I flew out of Carrickfinn Airport shortly after Mass, having said my good-byes. This time I did not weep. My heart was filled with gladness and thanksgiving for the gift of life and its felt abundance on this day. It was shot through by grace and by the rays of love, which the presence of the Risen Lord gave us to feel.

The heart can only bear so much at a given time, and for now this was enough!

Tinfoil and the Glory of God

God made my mother on an April day
From sorrow and the mist along the sea,
Lost birds' and wanderer's songs and ocean spray,
And the moon loved her wandering jealously.

Francis Ledwidge wrote this about his mother in 1915 when he was in hospital in Egypt. Now he has written again for my mother.

When I returned to Stonehill, I packed my garment bag with fresh clothes and hung it - open - on my bedroom door. It stayed there for practically the rest of the year. It was a daily reminder that, despite all the travelling I do in the course of the normal year, there was still another journey that would be the result of a single phone call from home.

I resolved that I would write down all the events that transpired while I was at home. That task was made easier because I had sent a daily e-mail bulletin to Fr. Bob Kruse, the executive vice-president at Stonehill, and fortunately he had not erased them. Most of what I wrote was a simple chronicle of events, but it was enough for my memory to clothe them with the Proustian sensibilities which made them part of a greater truth, the truth that includes the emotions and the heart.

My own mind was constantly swirling around the Easter experience, like a centrifuge that wanted to distill the elements, so that they might be carefully articulated. For me, it was a need to find meaning for myself - and perhaps hint at it for others - in the constant struggle towards the freedom to love simply, and to live that love in candid and transparent fashion. What set these thoughts in motion was our experience of my mother's simple life, that was graced in living and now in dying.

My emotional life was like a maelstrom during the time I spent at home. It occurred to me subsequently that had I been able to affirm my mother's prayer, I would have been carried into the heart of God. But I was neither able to pray with her, nor give any credit to the efficacy of her cry for life.

The whole episode came too quickly and I was unprepared. I had never heard anyone plead for their life before, except in movies and in television footage from Somalia, Kosovo, Burundi … wherever. Besides, I was quite used to my mother's reticence in the affairs of her soul. That is why the experience of her loud pleading made me cower in the shadows, my face buried in the eiderdown quilt that covered her bed.

Then I realized that perhaps all these thoughts were elaborate rationalizations for my cowardice, and that it was perhaps better to admit it and move on. Better to concentrate on what God was doing to her.

For us, the old Shaker hymn said it all:

> 'Tis the gift to be simple, 'tis the gift to be free,
> 'Tis the gift to come down where we ought to be,
> And when we find ourselves in the place just right
> 'Twill be in the valley of love and delight,
>
> When true simplicity is gained,
> To bow and to bend we shan't be ashamed,
> And turn, turn will be our delight,
> 'Til by turning, turning, we come round right.

There were so many of us, who were witnesses to the simplicity and the freedom, which were manifest in Maggie's life. What our eyes had seen and what our ears had heard, what our hands had clasped and our lips had suckled - this was our special witness of graceful simplicity. She had the freedom to be warm and joyful, kind and courageous, to be connection with hearth and home.

She was mother to us – and to many others as well.

That was undeniable. Not all of us said it, maybe not all of us thought it, but we envied her simplicity and wanted it – and the freedom that went with it. We knew the way to that freedom had to be difficult, but worth it. When we saw it before our eyes, it seemed like the pearl of great price.

My mother's prayer life was something constant that underlay every other thing you could say about her. Almost like a river that flows underground. One could become aware of the faint roar of water - *gurges ad gurgitem vocat, deep calls unto deep* - but there was nothing obvious to the eye that made her different. If anything, she blended with her surroundings like a chameleon, and she was always lively and full of fun. She was not passive-aggressive like some mothers of our race; she was as consistent in her moods as the Donegal rain.

When she was a girl, she and her sisters and brothers walked to the chapel in Bloody Foreland every Sunday for Mass. The chapel was actually at the back of the mountain, so it was called *Faoi Chnoc*, or *Under Hill*. The road from Meenacladdy was entirely uphill and even though the Master's children had shoes - good shoes for Sunday - they took them off and carried them in their hands for fear they would wear them out on the long journey to Sunday Mass and back. It took them at least five hours, without counting the time for Mass or dawdling on the way home.

While the schoolmaster's daughter was growing up to maturity in the second and third decades of the century, living a fairly secure life in the company of her siblings – they were left motherless when she was three – the man she was to marry later was having a different experience.

My father James McFadden was born in Gweedore - Lower Dore to be precise. His father was John McFadden, or John Thaidhg, as he was known by his patronym. He married a woman from the Rosses named Margaret McBride. She was referred to as Maragait Mhór (Big Margaret). Their circumstances were not comfortable. They had a large family, and even though their father was a small man, most of the children grew to be quite tall, men and women alike. It is said of Margaret Mhór that the day after childbirth, she would be out in the oat field behind the house putting up stooks of freshly mowed oats, with the new baby swaddled at the foot of one of the stooks. A woman's liberation to work the fields came early in those days.

When my dad and his brothers and sisters came of age, many of them had to seek seasonal employment in the Lagan. The customary way of doing this was to walk out through the glens to Letterkenny. There is still a structure to this day, a small bridge called *Droíchid a' Chaoineadh*, or *The Bridge of the Crying*. It is below Muckish Mountain, on the westerly side, and that was as far as their parents and siblings accompanied those who were leaving. Some of the older ones might be going to America, others going to Scotland, but the younger ones were going to *the Rabble Fair* in Letterkenny.

The *"Rabble Fair"* must have been a piteous sight, reminiscent in some ways of days before the Civil War in the American South. Fathers brought their young sons and daughters, barely fourteen, to be paraded in front of the farmers and shopkeepers of Ulster, the Lagan Valley in particular. Many of them came back to their families, but some did not. The young girls were referred to, as *"fine wee cutties"*, and after hiring, they were on their own. There was no one to monitor their care, or to teach them the things that young women ought to know. Young boys were supposed to know what was needful.

My father Jimmy was hired at one of the Rabble Fairs when he was only fourteen. The people who hired him owned a grocery store and pub in Belfast. He never said where, and we never asked. Indeed, he never spoke about the experience at all until the last year of his life when he was dying of cancer of the throat and mouth. When he recalled those years, he would say over and over again, *"Pure misery"!*

Apparently, he had to work from early morning in the shop and then in the pub until the last person had left - and still had to wash and polish the glasses for the next day. He said he was sometimes so tired that he fell asleep on the counter to be awakened when the first customers came in the next morning.

His experience explained many things about my dad's personality, his tendency to get manic at certain times and depressed at other times. I always felt that we were fortunate that he began to express these painful memories when he got closer to death. Had we known of them before, I think we might have been more understanding of him, because he did have a sensitive nature, and he tried to hide it from people. Hiding anything is an extra strain - and in the end it does not work.

Many things are hidden from children, and it is only when we realize that our parents were once young and had to fight *harder and more bitter battles than ourselves,* that we learn not to be so judgmental. We also learn that it is possible to forgive those whose moral or character flaws we think somehow responsible for our own unhappiness. Forgiveness is possible at any age, even for the dead. It is in our own best interest, now and later.

I do not know how long my dad worked in Belfast or what he did in subsequent years. At some point in his life he came to work in the Co-Operative store in Meenacladdy, and it happened that my mother was working there too. That is where they met. There is a wedding photograph of my parents in our living room in Calhame, and it shows my father who seemed taller in his youth, with an intelligent looking face - a bit reminiscent of Éamonn de Valera. My mother looks very young and lithe. The younger members of the family would remember her as older and more matronly because that is the way she was when we were born.

*　　*　　*　　*

> If you see me comin' better step aside
> A lot of men didn't, a lot of men died.
> St. Peter, don't you call me, 'cos ah cain't go,
> Ah owe mah soul to the company store.

Life would change radically for both my parents when they moved to Dungloe and dad became manager of the Co-op there. Dungloe was the center of the business life of the Rosses, and its importance was enhanced when the trains stopped coming to Burtonport, a few miles down the Coast Road.

One of the most famous people in the Donegal of my childhood was *Paddy-the-Cope*. He was called so, because Cope was the way the word Co-op was pronounced. And Paddy was famous because he had started the cooperative movement in Donegal even though he lacked any formal education.

The social and economic effect of cooperatives, not to mention the spiritual liberation it bestowed on the lives of ordinary people, was that it freed them from the gombeen man (from the Irish gaimbín, or *skulk*). The aforesaid species was one of our own kind, who played the entrepreneur with such skill that he kept the poor always in his debt. In some ways it was like the company store in some of the smaller industrial towns in America. You could never get out of its clutches because of your debt, and your debt, in turn, dictated that all your shopping had to be done there.

Landlords had brought this pernicious practice to perfection in the Ireland before the Land Wars. It had its counterparts in the social patterns of feudalism and serfdom in other parts of the world. The exchange of produce for rent reached inhuman levels during the reign of Queen Victoria, *The Famine Queen,* as she is known in Ireland. The failure of the potato crop for three successive years meant that the landlords resorted to eviction. In most cases they were dealing with *the wretched of the earth*, who were being evicted from huts of wattle and straw, and from the paltry little plots of land from which they scraped a semblance of livelihood.

The gombeen man carried on the same form of indenture in the small villages and towns. The country by now had been so depopulated by death and emigration, but the economic situation permitted the gombeen man to continue his sordid sway. It was the heroism of one man in our county - who though born poor, realized there had to be a better way than this - who conceived of starting the cooperative in rural Donegal.

Paddy the Cope's plan thrived and was copied elsewhere with great success, even in Canada, and some third world countries where Irish missionaries carried the idea with them. Towards the end of his life Paddy had become a celebrity, and the story of his crossing the Atlantic on the same ocean liner as Maureen O'Hara was on the front page of every Irish newspaper.

Paddy's autobiography was written with the encouragement of George Russell, a prominent figure in the Celtic Revival at the turn of the century. Russell wrote under the pen name of *(AE)*, and published a journal called *The Irish Homestead*. It was he who prepared the way for the cooperative movement when, on a visit to Dungloe, he addressed the farmers after Mass about the benefit they could gain by having a Co-Operative Agricultural Bank in the area.

What happened after that is told with great power of recall by Paddy the Cope in *My Story*. He humorously recalls that it was the inability of a colleague named Wright to pronounce Co-Op, and could only get as far as *Co-co-co - Cope*, that gave birth to the name. It is hard to believe that Harvard grads had same linguistic difficulties with their Co-Op, which has now become Coop, as in *chicken*.

While they were in Dungloe, my parents had a house on the Fair Hill, which was so named because the Fair was held there once a month. By this time, there were four children: Jim, Hughie, Margaret and Paddy. They had cousins in the town because my Uncle Charlie had married a widow with two children, and then had five of his own. He started the Rosses Cycle Depot on Carnmore Road and, after a few hard years made a great success of it.

Because my Uncle Charlie was older than my father, the young people in his family - John Joe, Cassie, James, Mona and Frances - were more mature than those in our family. Two of the girls, Mona and Frances, were especially devoted to my mother, and that became a life-long attachment. One of them explained that Maggie was not really that much older than themselves, and she was such a lively, fun-loving person that they considered her to be one of them. Thus, began a long tradition of entrusting their confidences to her, and coming to her with the usual teen dilemmas of parents who did not understand them, and affairs of the heart.

Our family moved to Calhame in 1930, probably because my grandfather had purchased a large house there, after the deaths of his children Bartley and Jean. Three of his other children, Sarah, Bridie and James - all grown and unmarried - came with him. They were to be as much a part of my growing up as my parents were, because all of us were in need of a place to be consoled when things got tough on us at home, the tough got going to Grandfather's house.

My parents began to build a house with a shop attached, and that was to be our home until we all scattered to the four winds in the early fifties. Breaking into a new market in the countryside was difficult because everyone already had their custom pledged to a certain grocer, not irrevocably of course, but in the world of country commerce allegiances, habits are hard to break.

When Jimmy was in his best form, he was very entrepreneurial. All the McFaddens must have inherited the same streak because three of dad's brothers and two of his sisters started enterprises of their own. For women to be in business at this stage of Ireland's history was unusual. What was more unusual was that none of them, men or women, had any background in the world of commerce.

One of the ways in which dad built up his customer base was to purchase a pony and a float. That allowed him to go from door to door, especially in Carrickfinn, which was fairly remote and was not served consistently by any of the existing grocery shops. This was the time when the tides met below at the beginning of the dunes, on the flatland that led to the peninsula.

Each of us children in their turn, sometimes two or three accompanied our father to Carrickfinn on Saturdays. We stopped at almost every house and the people would come out to the float, buy what they needed.

They would then sell whatever eggs or fish they had gathered for the week that had passed. Those who classify the way things are bought and sold, call this set of affairs *a barter economy*. Needless to say, we did not know that we were living in a barter economy - it all seemed perfectly ordinary to us.

There was a ritual to our Saturday. We spent extra time in some houses. In others, we took tea and ate bread with loads of salted country-butter. One of the Protestant homes had a huge illustrated Bible on the ledge of its front window. Needless to say, we took a peek, when Rachel and Fannie Boyd were out buying goods from dad or one of our brothers. We felt faintly sinful taking a look at a Protestant Bible, but we did it anyway because we did not have such grand books in our homes. We had to make do with the Bible Histories that were given out by Mrs. O'Donnell in school to augment what was contained in our catechisms.

Going to Carrickfinn was an all day affair, and it was nighttime when we came home. In the long winter evenings, it got dark early - and cold - especially when crossing the neck of the peninsula where there was no shelter. dad used to wrap us in his *cóta mór* (overcoat) or empty flour bags, or whatever was at hand. He would then put us into one of the several tea chests, which were emptied by then, and the pony would find his way home while dad went to make a delivery to an out-of-the-way house.

There was no grander way we could travel than in a tea chest. They came to us from London, or some other entrepôt, and they were filled with aromatic teas from Darjeeling or Ceylon. In addition to this, they were lined inside with tin foil and all of us children coveted tin foil because we could make shiny boats or planes out of it. Years after the tea-chest experience, I would learn that Gerard Manley Hopkins' writing long before my birth had made tin foil immortal, likening it in his poem, *God's Grandeur*, to nothing less than the glory of God: Hopkins writes:

> "The world is charged with the grandeur of God,
> It shall flame out, like shining from shook foil;
> It gathers to greatness, like the ooze of oil
> Crushed."

We had another reason for holding tea chests in the highest regard. When we asked the question that all children ask, *"Where did I come from?"*, in our house, at least, the answer was that we floated in from the sea in a tea chest. No child could imagine anything more shiny or grand. There were no stories about storks because they were not part of our lore and because we never saw any.

In any case, to ride on the back of dad's float from Carrickfinn was a special experience. We knew that Maggie would be there at the end of the journey and would lift us out in front of the kitchen's lighted windows, where we could smell the fresh pork bacon and sausage as we arrived on the street.

In the meantime, we were entrusted to our faithful pony Fannie who knew the way home. And we were securely tucked in a tea chest, listening to the loud roar of the ocean, and the gentle rustle of the tinfoil that lined the plywood tea-box. For us it was something that had sailed the seven seas - from the infinite ocean to the coast of Donegal where our parents were waiting for us.

Milking and cows a-bullin'

O Mary , go and call the cattle home,
And call the cattle home,
And call the cattle home,
Across the sands of Dee....

In 1986 I took a short sabbatical to Japan, China, Hong Kong and the Phillipines. On Thanksgiving Day I called my cousins in Yonkers, NY, since I always spent that day with them – my home away from home. Pat told me that Bella had gone home to Gweedore because her mother was dying. I changed my plans that day, left Manila and went home to Donegal via London and Belfast.

I was able to spend some time with my Dore cousins and with Aunt Mary who was very low. After greeting all her family on the first morning of her wake, I went back to London and then to New York on another unexpected journey.

While I was in Donegal, my good friend Phil Boyle died in Brooklyn. I had promised his wife Sarah before I left the United States that I would come from the deepest reaches of China - if I had to - when Phil died. His son James called me in Ireland to tell me of his father's death. He said they needed me and I should spare no cost in coming. I flew Concorde from London and the cheeky Immigration inspector at Kennedy Airport said, *"Do you mind if I ask you a question"*. Thinking it was another of the bizarre questions I am asked when I wear the Roman collar, I said, *"Of course not."* Then says he, *"How come a reverend like you can afford to fly Concorde"?* I told him I stole the money from last week's collection.

I had to be back at Stonehill by December 2nd because I had promised Deirdre Sullivan and Shaun Murphy that I would officiate at their wedding in the Ames mansion, which now houses mostly the College administration. At the small family reception, which followed their wedding, the couple gave me a gift. It was a watercolour by Martin Ahearn, an artist who used to exhibit summers in the Sheraton-Tara in Hyannis. It was a Donegal scene, the newly-weds said, and they hoped I would like it. When I unwrapped the painting, my eyes went out on two sticks.

Without knowing it, they had given me a painting of our own cow-byre, painted from the bridge below our house. There, in rust-red tin and stone stood MacFadden's cowshed, backed by the beautiful Donegal mountains and the sea-stream, running between the rocks and the strand in the foreground.

The grubby reality that was the subject of this lovely watercolour was razed to the ground this past year, but it lives on in the glory that art often bestows on nature. The building's finest hour was probably the day that dad brought a full-course Irish breakfast to Hannigan the tramp who spent the night sleeping in the hay. The condition was that Hannigan hand over his cigarettes and matches and that dad lock him in the hay-shed overnight. Hannigan's reaction to the breakfast was not recorded but after eating it, I presume he went back to sleep again.

Our byre was actually one of three sheds, stuck together, because they had been built at different times. It stood on a little neck of land that jutted out between our house and the tide. At one time, it stood behind Dunleavy's store, and Kitty Chaitlín's house. The building nearest the shore was the one which housed the animals, the one in-between was "The Store" where we kept the hay and bales of straw, and the low building, almost at Kitty's door was one where we sometimes kept hens and ducks - or pigs during the war.

When we were young, we dared not go near the byre alone because of Kitty Chaitlín who did not like our family. She had a dog, Cuskie, who ran after people who were crossing the strand in their bare feet, and sometimes bit them. She also had goats that stared at us with their small, beady eyes as they munched on leaves of sea holly on the other side of the stone wall where she had them tethered.

The nanny-goats were fairly bland looking, almost like sheep, but the billy-goats fascinated us because of the little goatees, *miogal* in Irish, which hung from their chins. Their gaze was definitely bolder than that of the nanny-goats, or the kids that accompanied them in the springtime. At our age, we had no reason to know that goats were randy, or that the Gospel used them to represent the damned. Looking back on it, it was probably their evil look that fascinated us. Some people said that when she died, Kitty wanted to be buried with her goats in the sally-rod garden across from her house. This did not do much for her reputation.

Sometimes, when Kitty's door was closed, we would venture up to the keyhole, and we could hear her clapping her hands and raving. Then we would run away as fast as our feet could carry us. The older children said when she was raving, she was putting a curse on our family. No one ever called her a witch, but in our childhood we believed that a person had the power to curse (*mallacht*), or to bless (*beannacht*).

The curses are still preserved in the language and they are examples of Celtic oxymoron, the purest of maledictions, that call on no one less than God to bring the evil result. *"Scrios De ort!"* or *"God's curse to you"* is still the most potent curse that can be called down upon a person for perceived wrong, or vengefulness. No one knows if it has an effect, but at the same time no one likes to be on the receiving end of the *"Scrios De"*!

It was not hard to believe that Kitty had the power to curse and that she used it liberally. If you had the misfortune to cross her at the village pump, she would just as likely dump a bucket of water over your head, despite her age, and seeming infirmity.

Kitty and her dog and her rantings were like the three Billy Goats Gruff that we had to pass every day as we went to the byre, to let the cows and calves out to graze. Sometimes we had to take them to different fields for pasture, sometimes we had to tether them, and after school we usually herded them until the evening - which never came too soon.

Then we would take them home and make sure that they were firmly tied in their stalls. Maggie always milked the cows morning and evening, and oftentimes one or other of us went with her to help her carry the cans of milk home, because the yield was heavier in evening - especially when the cows had recently calved.

But we went to the byre for other reasons too, and sometimes those reasons had nothing to do with helping Maggie. We knew it was a good time to get permission to go to a film or a dance, probably after dad had said *no*. But we also liked to watch her milking the cows with such a firm and gentle rhythm.

She was always patient and good with the animals, even when they were restless. When they would either kick or try to hit her in the face with their tails, she would always manage to calm the cows down before she did anything else. Then she would massage their udders with her hand to clean them of burrs or thistles or any other detritus that they had picked up from being in the fields all day.

Sometimes she would let us try to milk, but when we squeezed the cow's teat, nothing would come out. It was amazing to see how she could get such a long *'steall'* or *'squirt '* from the cow's udder, using both hands to milk the teats into the bucket cradled between her legs. We soon learned that you had to pull and squeeze in the same movement to be a good milker. We even learned the barnyard art of squirting.

John remembers how mother could direct one of these squirts into our open mouths, and all he can think of now is that it was *'unpasteurised milk'*. But at that time no one knew about those things. All that was important was that you kept your animals clean, and that you had a clean household to store the milk, a cool room in which to keep the clotted cream until the time came to churn it.

Then it was time for huge patties of country butter made with paddle-sticks and cold water and lots of coarse salt. Some people had decorative molds, which gave the butter an elegant look; but with or without the decorations, homemade butter was bliss to the palate of hungry children.

*   *   *   *

Spending time with mother while she was milking was not always an unselfish matter, even though most of the time we were there to help her. Sometimes we were there because we found her alone. Maybe it was her contented bliss that made us sense the right time to confide in her, or own up to something that we would rather do face to face.

It was in the cow-byre that I told her I was going away to study for the priesthood. I was almost eighteen at the time and I don't recall that she stopped her milking at my announcement. She knew that from the Easter of my freshman year, I had kept first place in my class at *Coláiste Éinde* in Galway, and that I would be offered a scholarship from one of the branches of the National University.

Obviously, I had changed my mind about being a physician or a research chemist, and she was the first one I told. I know she was pleased, but maybe not surprised. She was ready to affirm us in all of our decisions, and consequent to that, she would have prayed that they were wise decisions.

When the more generous flow of milk would stop, mother would make the rounds of the teats several times, to make sure she had emptied them. *Milking* anything has given its name as metaphor for getting the last possible drop, but mother's motivation was not greed in this case. It was to leave the animal comfortable, and to insure that no infection would set in if milk were left standing in the animal's udder.

A cow was an important animal in any house during the war years, and we usually had two of them and a couple of calves or sturrocks at any given time. We generally kept the calves that were born in that byre. If they were bull calves, we usually sold them after a few years, and if they were heifers we would keep them for ourselves. mother gave names to the different animals. We had a dusky looking cow in the sixties that she called *Sadat*, after Anwar Sadat, who was President of Egypt at the time.

Sadat had a bull calf and we left him too long without castration, so he mounted his mother in the fields one day, and got her pregnant. The issue of this incestuous union was a bull-calf to whom mother gave the name *Clement*. She said she named it for Clement Freud, grandson of the great Sigmund, who was serving as MP in the British Parliament at Westminster. mother knew little of Greek tragedies or Freudian oedipal complexes - at least, so we thought - till Sadat had her son's calf.

When we were old enough, we were allowed to assist our cows at their calving. This was an event that was always eagerly awaited because we loved to see newly- born calves or foals, pups or kittens - anything that was tiny and that we could stroke or cuddle. After a while we became expert at knowing all the signs that proceeded a calving, and while we were not allowed to deliver the calf, we often held the flashlights that helped my brothers see what they were doing in the darkness of the byre.

I will always remember the first time Tadhg, who was the baby in our family, was allowed to see one of our cows calving. When he saw the calf's tiny feet appearing - after the water was broken - his eyes went out on two sticks. The process that followed was fairly arduous, and it sometimes took an hour or so, with the use of rope tied around the calf's front legs to make sure the head came out first. After that, the rest of the calf slid out easily. All Tadhg kept saying during this time, much to our amusement, was, *"But Mama, how did he manage to get in there?"*

*   *   *   *

He would soon find out, because in a few years he would have to help take the cow to the bull. The bull in our area was a bull kept by the Boyds - down past the lake in Carrickfinn. When a cow is in heat, or as the local people say, when she's *a-bullin*, she will not stay grazing quietly or chewing her cud. She will roar a lot, get frothy at the mouth and become very difficult to manage.

Despite what nature desires for her, she is not inclined to go anywhere easily, has to be roped and almost dragged to Boyd's house in Carrickfinn. It usually took three fairly strong lads to accomplish this, one with a rope to lead her and two with sallyrods behind her. Once at the Boyd's house she would be made to stand still, until the bull was led out from its enclosure. The bull would then do some sniffing and pawing at the ground, while he began to lather and get aroused.

We were not allowed to do anything at this stage of the game, except hold the cow in place as best we could, and help her to brace for the coming encounter. The bull who was more than eager, and had begun to drip in anticipation, was controlled by his handlers - usually Guy or Joe Boyd - with a rope that ran through a ring in his nose. He was carefully guided to the cow.

The coupling that took place was awkward because of the bull's weight and the fact that he usually could not see what he was doing. Often one of the adults would have to guide his penis to the right place. When he had finished doing his thing, the cow would relax and her back would go upwards in a hump. She was then *"bulled"*, and could be led quietly up the banks, and back to our byre again. We rarely had to go back to the bull a second time.

Someone once said that all of Edna O'Brien's novels had only one theme - *"virginity and barnyard lust"*. We had experienced both before we knew what they were - even before they were either lost or acquired. While they were *"learning experiences"*, we always knew the important thing: that we had a new calf on the way, and that it would be a great boon in a few years to our family and to our grandfather's house with which we shared the bounty of milk and cream, and the patties of country butter.

*   *   *   *

There were things in every household that were very important during the years of the war. The death of an animal - especially a milk cow – was a heavy financial loss for any family, because no one had the savings to replace it with another. There was usually a bout of sharing until a calf grew to milk-bearing age, or until a family scrimped and saved to buy a new cow at Jack's Fair, held in Meenaleck. We never knew who Jack was, but we were often at his fair.

So it was not for any mundane reason that when mother finished milking, she would put her finger in the milk-froth and make the sign of the cross on the cow's side. *'Coisreacadh Dé ort, a bhó bhocht!*

God's *blessing on you, dear cow!'* she would say at the end of every milking, and on her way home she would spill a little milk into the good earth, to give thanks for its generosity.

In earlier times, spilling the milk was an offering to the *'little people'*, as I learned from Séan Haughey, a master-collector of Irish folklore all his life. These offerings were obviously still in the memory of the people and known as *pisreógaí. mother* was not into *pisreógs*, but after milking, she would transform the same act with another motivation.

At a time of great pain in his own life, it was the image of Maggie milking the cows that came to my brother Tadhg's mind, and around which he composed a poem which he sent to me. It was a tribute to a peace he had once known and which was now eluding him. He gave me this years before Maggie's death. I kept the poem so that I could write verse of it here:

> A candle glowing in a byre
> While she, who radiates security?
> Dips
> A finger in the frothy milk
> To bless the provider.
> Silence, songs and words of kindness
> For a beloved cow.
> Love abounds in the heavy
> Manure-laden air
> The candle is snuffed.

There is a second verse about his pain, but it is only his remembered peace that is germane here.

A Woman of the Islands

Báidín Fhéilimi, d'imithi go Torai,
Báidín Fhéilimi, 's Féilimi ann
Báidín Fhéilimi , briseadh 1 dTorai
Báidín Fhéilimi 's Féilimi ann.
(Phelimy's boat went into Torry.
Phelimy's boat and Phelimy in it.)
Donegal sea-shanty

The only grandparent I ever knew was my mother's father. He had a big house next to ours and he lived there with my aunts, Sarah and Bridie, and my Uncle James. Since our house was always busy, the Big House - as it was known - was a pleasant place to visit. Down in the parlor which was filled with interesting things, there hung a portrait of a beautiful looking woman, clothed in black with a white blouse that mounted to her neck, asserted by a two small cameo brooches. Her dark hair was massed above her head; she had fine features, eyes, nose and mouth - in perfect proportion. We knew she was our grandmother, Brigid Doohan (Ó'Dubhchóin), and that she was born in Thorraí Island, nine miles off the northwest coast of Donegal.

My mother hardly ever spoke of her. That was not unusual because my father never spoke of his parents either. But you expect more background chat from your mother about these things - even if you are not terribly interested - because mothers are the bearers of family tales in a way that fathers are not. We got the sense that this lovely Grandmother was connected to sorrow. As Francis Ledwidge says about his own mother, *"there was that in her that always mourned"*.

When we asked mother about the lady in the portrait, she said she had no memories about her own mother. She had died after giving birth to my Uncle James and our grandfather, Séamus Duggan (Ó Dubhgáin), was left with a houseful of children to rear on his own. He did not marry again.

After the course of my mother's illness, I decided I wanted to find our more about her mother's people, so I announced one day that I was going to Thorraí. I had been there once before with Jim and Margaret, but then we were only interested in seeing the island. Pádraig MacRúairí, *"Rí Thoraigh"* or King of Thorraí was still alive on that occasion, and he entertained my sister Martha and myself while Jim and the others went exploring the area of the higher sea-cliffs. We also visited the hut of Derek Hill, the famous landscape painter who has spent a great deal of his life on the island. This time, I had something else on my mind. John and his son Danny said they would come with me.

We reached the pier before noon. A few people had gathered for the journey and, as we looked around, there was a fair amount of activity taking place. The ferryboat was still on its way back from the island. When it arrived we could see that it carried a large number of tourists. The turnaround time was remarkable because the ferry disgorged its passengers quickly, and just as quickly took aboard those of us on the pier, who had grown to be quite numerous by now.

I found it quite amazing that so many people would be heading for an island whose name was synonymous with *remoteness* for years - and even centuries. *Toraigh na dTonn* (Torry of the Waves) was still a place that was constantly emerging from the mists of mythology, and its very location almost defied history to lay a glove on it. Perhaps it was this that attracted people to it. There is a special awe that draws people to the ragged edge of the western world, and to the chaos that lies beyond it.

With the last batch of goods aboard, the ferry nudged itself away from the pier, turned when the water was deep enough and headed for the island. We did not have a clear view of Thorraí as we departed because another island, Inishboffin, (The Island of the White Cow) lay between us - a little to the north.

When we cleared the south end of Inishboffin, the massive granite fortress of Thorrai lay before us, opalescent and gray. Now it was a battleship that set sail on midsummer's night, now it was the shape of legends, home of the Fomorian pirate race - the fastness of Balor of the Evil Eye, the place where St. Columcille's crook landed - a quarter not remote enough for the saint's self-imposed exile, and which he quit for Iona of the Scots.

To be in Thorraí Sound is to feel the Atlantic in its full force almost any day, to see the waves of the Gulf Stream that wash through the Sound on its way to Scotland and the Shetlands – our life-giving connection with the warm waters of the Mexican Gulf. To turn around to capture the sight of all the Donegal headlands, from north to south, humping their way to the ocean is something that should not be reserved for a day. It was enough beauty for a lifetime, as Rilke remarks in one of his Duino elegies: *"Earth, my dearest... O believe me, you no longer need your springtimes to win me over – one of them, ah, even one, is already too much for my blood...."*

Níl contae in Éirinn níos deise na thú
Níl daoini sa domhan mhór níos mó a fuair cliú;
Ná mbar bhí i dTír Chonaill abhus agus thál
Ó grá geal mó chroí thú, mo shean Dún naGall...

-(love song to Donegal)

We were already at the Thorraí pier, looking at the passengers gathered for the ferry's return. Big James was operating a crane on the site, massing a foundation of sea stones and sand to fill the concrete box that would extend the pier further into the sea. We saw Paul Rodgers, our cousin, waiting for us in the crowd and soon he was greeting us with kisses and showering us with words of welcome to the island.

We were his first catch of the day, and he insisted that the first visit should be to his home. His wife Mary, a nurse whom he met and wed in Dublin, greeted us at the door. While she served us tea and sandwiches, Paul began to sing for us, pausing after every second verse to renew his welcome for us and thanking us for the honour of our company. My nephew Danny, a tall lanky sixteen-year-old, was chuffed no end to find himself addressed and included in Paul's honorific language which was nothing if not inclusive.

After the singing, Paul drew his accordion up on his knee, and proceeded to play for us, *con brio*, a medley of tunes, new and old. We sat in total fascination not only at the entertainment, but that it was being provided to us at *high noon*. Paul was not the only one who was enraptured by his own performance.

I looked at Mary to see how this was going down with her, and what I saw was a look of love and adoration for her Paul. This fascinated me more than Paul's playing, and I could not help think what a lucky man he was to have met and courted her and brought her back to his native island. When I told my sister Margaret about my impression later that day, she nodded in assent because the same devotion had caused her wonderment too.

For a while, I harbored a fleeting fear that Paul would be our company for the whole time, but his host instinct was not lacking. At the right time, he acknowledged that our stay on the island would be short and he escorted us to Jenny's house. Jenny was sitting by the fire, and she rose to greet us when we entered. She was the one that held the most interest for my brother John, and it did not surprise me that he had met her before.

Jenny was the one whom we had really come to see. In a glance, I could easily see in her face my mother's features and those of several cousins. I half-knew what to expect, but even if I didn't, there was no mistaking. It had the same features as the face of my Island grandmother in Grandfather Duggan's house: the soft skin, the dark hair, the hazel eye. All of it came together, and there was no need to be introduced.

John did most of the talking after we shook hands with Jenny and her son Hughie Óg. John was intent on having her confirm a story that he had heard several years before in Magheraroarty from an old woman who was on her deathbed. She had told him told him that the Thorraí family referred to on the Island as the *"Sally Alecs"*, was the one to which my Thorraí grandmother belonged. She was descended on the maternal side from the Olpherts, the old woman said.

The Olpherts - in their time - were the landlords of Thorraí and the whole mainland swath of territory, from Knockfola to Dunfanaghy.

It was said among the islanders that one of Lord Olphert's daughters had fallen in love with a fisherman from Thorraí who had reason to frequent the Olphert estate in Ballyconnell, most likely to supply them with fish. Despite the distress that this caused her family, she married the fisherman and went to live with him in Thorraí.

When her father followed her into the island, and failed to have her renounce her Papist nuptials, he agreed to build a house for herself and her fisherman husband, but told her that she would be cut off from her family forever.

Jenny confirmed for us that this was the story of her maternal forebears. My grandmother and she belonged to the *Sally Alecs*. It was the only family on the island where the names Jennie and Alec were found, typical Scots names, forms of Jean and Alexander, Alec, Alistair and Sandy, that were not indigenous to the Irish-speaking islanders of Thorraí.

John had gone to the trouble of looking up the Olphert family tree, in his interest to verify this story. The only thing he could find there was the name of one of Lord Olphert's daughters who was listed with no issue, and with no date of birth or death. She was alone in having no annotation attached to her name. We are still looking for this link, but perhaps it will never be discovered.

There will always be an invitation to mystery in the deep hazel eyes of grandfather's *last duchess hanging on the wall.*

A Mountainy Schoolman

"Beside yon straggling fence that skirts the way,
With blossom'd furze unprofitably gay,
There, in his noisy mansion , skilled to rule
The village master taught his little school...
Amazed the gazing rustic ranged around;
And still they gazed, and still their wonder grew,
That one small head could carry all he knew."

-Oliver Goldsmith

Séumas Duggan the grandfather whom we called *Morning* as a pet name because he was the only one who said *"Good Morning"* to the children in our house when this greeting would have been unusual - was from the Donegal Rosses, from a place called Bun, at the foot of the Mullaghderg mountains. *Bun (at the foot of)* is a word like *Tor (high place).* To pronounce it properly, you almost have to have to expel it from your mouth at the speed of a bullet and then try to pull it back in again in the same breath.

Morning came from a family of people who were known as *"the Pártláns"* because the name Pártlán (or *Bartley*) ran all through his forebears - the papa bears, the mama bears and the baby bears. Even though I am a bearer of the name, strictly speaking, I am not a *Pártlán,* because it belongs with the O'Dubgáin name.

Often I am asked why I have such an English-sounding name like *Bartley* and I point out that it is the first recorded name in the pre-historic Ireland. The first invasion was by a man named Partolán, and his followers were called Partalonians. There is a mixture of Semitic *(bar)* and Egyptian *(Ptolemy)* in the name, and it might argue for a Phoenician colonization.

In any case the *Pártláns* owned a good stretch of bogland according to the Land Commission records, but I never got the impression that these families were well off. Bogland, after all, is not very productive except for peat, or peat moss. Neither were in hot demand at the time my grandfather was growing up.

*   *   *   *

The house where *Morning* was born is a ruin now. The ivy-covered stones of a ruined gable are all that's left – a good place for nesting blackbirds. Someone built a cowshed off the other gable, but I had no desire to explore it. Anyway, a rather large cow stood in the doorway, and she looked too formidable for me to move her.

On the evening I went to visit the ruin, the sky above me was filled with ominous dark blue clouds. I thought a cloudburst might be in the offing when, suddenly, a shaft of light, like a giant floodlight coming from the setting sun - which I could not see - lit up the bottom of the clouds, and burnished them the colour of gold. The transformation of a menacing cloud to a dazzling bright floodlight gave me an idea of what I might see if I climbed the two ridges above the ruins in the little hollow.

My lungs were puffing from the exertion when I reached the top, but my heart began to pound even more from the beauty that lay on every side. I could see the Bluestack Mountains to the southeast, and from there to the northeast an arc of sea and rockbound shore, islands, mountain lakes, hill and heathland, lovely at sunrise and breathtaking at sunset. If my grandfather could live off beauty, he would be richer than Bill Gates or the Sultan of Brunei. That was not the case, but one likes to think that, at least, it might have fired his imagination and fed his dreams to develop his own talent.

*   *   *   *

In 1831, a letter from Lord Stanley to the Lord Lieutenant of Ireland established elementary schools. They were called *National Schools,* and before them existed the hedge-schools of which we have only fragmentary records. The Catholic Church was at first reluctant to take advantage of the schools, fearing another trap by the British Government, but other groups were not so slow to move into the gap; so it was, that the *the proselytzing schools* - as they were referred to - came into being.

There was a great population of unchurched Irish (it is hard to guess at their spiritual condition) and this group was looked on as fair game by the Methodist, Presbyterian and Anglican Churches of Ireland.

To put things in perspective: it is still only a few years after the 1828 Emancipation of Catholics; the Great Hunger has not happened yet, and the population of Ireland is huge, approximated at 8.1 to 8.3 million people. This figures still boggles my mind every time I think of it. It conjures up the Netherlands and clog shoes, or even the fields of China - black with peasants in every field and rice-paddy.

Eventually, as the Catholics became less wary, and after the population was decimated, National Schools began to be built throughout the counties. Obviously, they could not all be built at once. The oldest that I know of in our area is Thorr School, which goes back to 1872.

To become a schoolmaster in my grandfather's time, at the end of the last century, was a great accomplishment. Pupils who showed promise in the National Schools were appointed as *Monitors* and allowed to teach the younger classes for a year or two. Then they sat for the *King's Scholarship* which got them a coveted place at one of the teacher-training colleges. *Morning* went to the *De La Salle College* in Waterford for his training.

When he was finished training, Séamus Duggan got Tor (or Thorr) as his first school. Tor (high place) deserves its name, if nothing else. Even today it is a place of great and splendid isolation, because it is in the uplands of the Donegal, and one wonders why the British administration ever built a school there. The only reason I can surmise is that Thorr was at the confluence of several valleys and - in a strange way - accessible to all in the trackless moorland.

Two prominent Irish-Americans are linked to the place despite its remoteness. Dr. Tony O'Reilly, former CEO of the Heinz Co. of Pittsburgh, and founder of the American-Ireland Fund, was sent to Thorr summers to learn Irish under the tutelage of the McMonagles who were schoolteachers there. Dr. Michael Roarty, master marketing-strategist for Anheuser-Busch, had also visited there with his father from the time he was seven.

Tony does not remember his summers there fondly, because of the loneliness. Michael, whose father was born in *Mín-na-Mánrach,* loved his visits because Donegal was heaven compared to Detroit. In any case, there were lots of good people who were born and reared in Thorr. Some of them were well-off compared to the coastland folk because they could have large flocks of sheep on the mountain. Minimal maintenance, and the sheep could roam into the mist-covered mountains - not to be seen again till *dipping* time or *lambing* time came around again.

Soon, the loneliness of Tor will be prized only by those who need the wilderness to talk to God.

* * * *

Thor School was accessible, after a fashion. There was only one road in the Rosses at the time - and that road was built in the second year of the Great Hunger. *Fionn MacCumhaill* writes in his book, *Na Rosa Go Brách*, that one man was hired from every house to work on the road and on Fridays they were paid with a little tub of corn meal, also known as *maize* or *Indian meal*. From that time onwards the road was known as *Beálach na Mine Buí (the Road of the Yellow Meal)*. For the rest, there were bridle paths and tracks - and tracks give comfort only because they indicate that someone has gone that way before.

Morning used to take his shoes in hand and hike over the heather-covered bogland, from *Bun* to *Tor*, with a boiled egg in his pocket for lunch. He returned home the same way every evening. A few years later, he got a school in a place called *Mín a' Chladaigh*. With the school came a fine house, the best in the whole neighbourhood.

According to the accounts, Meenacladdy was a fairly well settled area at the time. There was a triangle of flat land, almost a glen, wedged in between the mountains but open to the coast and to the area called *"the Mines,"* where there was once a short-lived lode of silver discovered. It was thus accessible from several directions.

Living on the eastward coast of the Atlantic Ocean had its grander moments; it also had its drawbacks. One of the drawbacks was the constant exposure to wind, rain, squalls, and – occasionally

– gales and storms that rival hurricanes in their destructive potential. Consequently, all the houses - long and thatched and whitewashed- were built with a solid wall to the ocean side, and doors and windows to the landward side. Having a view of the ocean and the islands was not desirable, because there were days of the year when one's doors or windows could literally be blown in.

The Meenacladdy School in which *Morning* taught is long gone. But the schools were all built on the same plan, depending on the population. There were usually two or three rooms, large windows, fireplaces, and a row of unkempt and foul privies out back. Game facilities were nil, but the children were sent outside for vigorous exercise of their own several times a day. They usually played games of *"chasing"* each other around the schoolyard. They often had to bring sods of turf (peat) with them from home to heat the schools in the winter. That continued up until my own time, but now there is central heating in all the schools.

In my mother's childhood, the first decades of the 1900's, there was still an expectation that local teachers and parents would collaborate with the authorities in fostering English and suppressing Irish. Sticks and other emblems were worn by the children, or kept in the school or home, to gauge the use of Irish by the children. These emblems were sometimes called *score-sticks* or *tally-sticks*. In Irish they were called bataí, cípíní scóir, or *capaill bhána*. These were to be marked or notched by parent or teacher when a child spoke Irish, and the child was to be punished accordingly.

The following day at school, punishment was meted out for breaching the linguistic law. mother told us that she had to wear one of these wooden *signums* around her neck, and I often wondered how her father could bring himself to punish her, or any of his other children, for that matter, for speaking Irish. But there were visits from inspectors to examine the notches, and I suppose something had to be produced to show that the Meenacladdy School was modestly compliant, and had its modest share of culprits.

Mother once told a story of two boys who had a memorable meeting with her father, Master Duggan. *Morning* went to Heúdi's house to buy some seed potatoes, and there he saw two boys who had never been to school. Naturally, he was surprised to see them, and grilled them about why they did not come to school. He told them they had better show up on Monday or he would send the police after them.

When *Morning* was leaving Heúdi's house with the potatoes he came to buy, he heard one of the boys say to the other, *"Is daor a ceannuigh muidinne cuid preatai Heúdi / How dearly ' us ones' paid for Heudi's potatoes."*

Morning must have told this story often because it was part of mother's lore. When she told this story, she would always marvel at the rich turn of phrase in Irish the boys used - to describe the value-added cost that derived from their meeting with the schoolmaster. She would marvel again at the idea that two young unschooled boys had such a command of Irish to express themselves so eloquently about their ill-fated meeting with their soon-to-be schoolmaster who came to buy their father's seed-potatoes. Anyone with an appreciation for Irish will know what a linguistic jewel this phrase is - and then think it was to be beaten out of them in the name of education!

*   *   *   *

Grandfather could see his own house from his school window and, after his wife died, his eldest daughter Mary was put in charge of the house. She was an extremely generous person. She was also probably too young to have that kind of responsibility. She attracted some friends from the neighbourhood, something that was not lost on her father, the Master Duggan, who had more than his schoolroom in focus while he was teaching.

At dinner, my mother said, conversation would sometimes be turned in Mary's direction:

- Goidé bhí Sarah Bhilly ag cuartú uait inniú?
  What was Sarah Bhilly asking from you today?

- Bhí sí ag cuartú rud beag plúr le h-arán a dhéanú.
  She was looking for a little flour to make bread.

- Agus goidé bhí cuir bhuarthú are Annie Pháidi?
  And what was troubling Annie Phaidi ?

- Rud beag olive oil fá choinne a cuid gruaig!
  She wanted a little olive oil for her hair!

The list went on - and it was not recorded how long Mary lasted as the quartermaster of the house, but she was soon to be replaced by Sarah, the next oldest, who was not such an easy touch.

This was not to suggest that my grandfather was a miser, but his provisions would have been only relatively greater to the vast mass of people who were poor, and he had a large family himself, and no wife to help him. mother said he was very good to beggars and those in need, and she recalled him once even giving the shoes off his feet to a tramp who crossed the strand barefoot in his company, but who had to go farther . . . as *Morning* turned into his house at the end of the strand.

*   *   *   *

> "Fare thee well, my little Indian maid,
> Fare thee well, my Indian star...
> I will come again to see you
> On the coast of Malabar"

The standing of the schoolmaster in the townland was considerable. People came to him to read letters that they had received from America, and to compose replies. They came also for help in responding to the various authorities that ruled their lives. They came for advice about where a gifted child might go after primary school, for advice about financial difficulties - or even about their cattle or sheep.

My grandfather was not remembered as being especially political, but he could not avoid being caught up in the events of the Easter Rising, the rise of the Irish Republican Army - the world's first guerilla movement against England, the partition of Ireland, and the subsequent Civil War between Éamonn DeValera and Michael Collins, the assassination of Collins, and the rise to power by DeValera.

As a child attending political rallies, I knew that people had taken sides but what they were about was lost in the mists of my pre-existence. I knew it was all right to tear down the posters of DeValera and the *Fianna Fáil* party that other families put on the telephone poles. They tore our *Fine Gael* posters down too, so all was fair at election time. It added more passion to our otherwise exciting lives in the country.

The rallies that attended one candidate or another were usually held outside the Church gate, because it was the only place they could be assured of an audience taken captive. It was not uncommon to hear some partisan yell at another, "*Where were you in 1916?*" as if that were the touchstone for being a true Irishman.

We never asked dad, "*What did you do in the war, daddy?*" because we did not think he was very much involved. Maggie said he carried a gun for a few nights on Crolly Bridge, and we took that laconic comment as an indication that he belonged to the *"other side"*. Maggie, in any case, was a Free Stater and stayed that way until she died. She loved Garrett Fitzgerald and had no great love for Charlie Haughey. She would argue the toss at anytime with my brother Tadhg, about the merits of either leader. She was a keen follower of politics, and she always regarded Tadhg as having been seduced by Fianna Fáil. That meant that he had been led astray from his true patrimony, the only one in our family to stray in the wrong direction.

The famous Civil War *was about a real issue,* but like many other civil wars, *it was also a chance to settle local grudges.* Because *Morning,* my grandfather, had authority over the school building in Meenacladdy, the IRA once asked him for the use of the school for one of their meetings. They left the schoolhouse in such disrepair that, the next time they asked him, he answered with a firm *'No'.*

Soon after he was kidnapped and held in a little sheep *cró* (hut) up in the mountains for several days. mother said the galling part was that it was his own former students who did this. She recalled the terror his disappearance struck into the hearts of his motherless children, and how her sister Sarah and she walked the several miles to Derrybeg during the night to tell the parish priest that their father had been taken away.

The priest may have been aware of the fact already, but he told them to go back home and not to worry because their father would be back home soon. The priest probably had to crack a few heads to accomplish this, but I am sure that given the times, the local thuggery, and the political sophistication, no elaborate diplomacy was needed.

The experience of being kidnapped and held captive had a traumatizing effect on *Morning.* Not surprising for anyone who has lost their freedom for even a short time. Uncertainty can send the mind and emotions into a tailspin. The perpetrators of *Morning's* kidnapping would have added to the trauma.

Some time afterwards, he went missing at an important event in his parish, probably Confirmation, which would have involved his school and all the other schools in the parish area of Gortahork. After his absence was noted, they began to look for him, and − he was found, fairly intoxicated from *poteen,* in the little hut in the mountains where he was taken prisoner. He was only an occasional drinker, but this was an indication of how severely traumatized he was by the kidnapping. The only possible explanation for his behavior was that he must have returned to re-live the events - attempting to rid his mind of the hurt.

*   *   *   *

There was a sidebar to this event. He did not trust the local people much after that, and did not mix with them anymore. After all he did in the area - as a help to everyone - it probably rankled him greatly that former students could be so mean over a political cause.

Morning quickly became friends with the Dixons of Meenlara who had a large house attached to a grocery and bar. They were genial and friendly people who kept islanders for weeks on end when the seas were too high for them to return home.

Dixons was a hub for everyone, and most especially for the people of Inisboffin and Thorraí, when they came out to buy provisions and sell their fish. It was here that Morning came in contact with the Thorraí people for the first time, and it was from the pier below Dixons that he made his first trip to the island. No one knows how he came in contact with the young Brigid Doohan. It is possible that someone made a match for him.

In any case, the second time Séumas Duggan went into the island, it was to take her back as his wife. They both had the same root to their names in Irish − Dubhgáin and Dubhchoin. Dubh is the word for black and there was no doubt that they carried the genes to justify the name. And no, they were not the *"black Irish"*, as this is commonly understood in America, that is, people who have Spanish or Norman or even Sicilian blood in their veins. There is explanation aplenty for the dark Irish from the fact that the Norse invaders had a go at our coastline, especially in the Northwest, in the centuries before the first millenium.

The Irish themselves distinguished between the Dubh-ghall or the *dark foreigner* - probably Norwegian - and the Finn-ghall or *fair foreigner* - probably Danish.

Dark or fair, there was a strong streak of Viking red in other coastland families whose blood had been thinned by the barbarian.

* * * *

Children of the Raven

The first to get up
Will be mother…We'll hear her
Quietly laying the fire,
Quietly putting the kettle on the stove
And cosily taking the teapot out of the cupboard
We'll be home once more.

- Vladimir Holan

Morning and his wife had eight children: Mary, Sarah, Bartley, Jennie, Hugh, Bridie, Maggie, and James. My grandmother died giving birth to James, and my grandfather was left with a young family to rear and teach by himself. He never married again.

Mary went to America to marry a young man, Eddie Curran, without her father's approval. She worked for several years in a New York hotel where Charlie Chaplin was a frequent guest. She remembered him as the hardest man to please she ever ran across.

Once Chaplin called the manager of the hotel to complain about the sheets that Aunt Mary had ironed and put on his bed. In front of her, he demanded they be removed because he could see creases in them. That day the manager braved the ire of Chaplin, and vindicated Aunt Mary, insisting that the sheets were perfectly fine. Chaplin threw a tantrum, but it did no good.

Sarah and Bridie and James stayed with their father for the rest of his life. After his death, Bridie went to work at King's College in

Newcastle-on Tyne, while James went to a place called Oldham in England. Sarah stayed at home and looked after anyone who needed looking after. She looked after many of the younger children around the houses in Calhame - often whether they liked being looked after or not.

Bartley became a steward on the Cunard Lines, sailing out of Liverpool to Halifax and New York. He died young and is buried in an unknown grave in Liverpool. The cause of death was fever of some kind, but he was buried before news of his death reached home. My mother used to say that *Morning* cried long and hard for the son he had named after his own father. He was not to be consoled, my mother said, because this son was his favourite.

Jennie went to Dublin to become a nurse in the years when the *Black and Tans* were terrorizing the country, and she returned home suffering from tuberculosis, or *consumption,* as they called it at that time. Actually, while she was ill, the *Black and Tans* broke into the flat she was sharing with another girl, frightened them but did not harm them. Jenny was buried in a grave of some friends, because the family was too new to Annagry parish to have a plot of their own in the local graveyard.

Hugh became a teacher like his father. He was dark like his mother, a handsome man who favoured black suits, white shirts, and a black bow tie in the classroom and in public. He was extremely intelligent, and in some ways wasted on elementary schoolchildren. He was like my grandfather in many ways - patient and gentle at times - especially when he was explaining a difficult question in maths or geometry. He could also be tempestuous - almost imperious - at other times when things did not go his way. Even then, he looked magisterial.

Uncle Hugh and my mother were very close. It was clear that she and her sisters worshiped *"Hughie Mór"*, as they called him. He was, after all, the only one who carried on the link between the Duggan family and higher education. His friends referred to him as *"An Dubhgánach"*, which is the singular honorific of his family name, as if he represented the whole clan. In many ways he did - and he was the last intellectual beacon of the name.

My mother sent me to his school in Dóbhar for four years to be tutored in Irish and other subjects. Uncle Hugh was very good to me, but always had me apart from the regular classes because he gave me special work to do. I often think of myself as going to an intensive-learning school because it was mostly former exam papers he gave me to do. The papers were those set for entrance into the Preparatory Schools which prepared the nation's teachers.

I don't remember who made the decision to send me to Uncle Hugh's school for tutoring. It wasn't because our own school was deficient, but the instruction was mostly in English which meant that the Irish of the students was fairly spotty, even though some of them would have parents who spoke Irish at home. At Uncle Hugh's house, I lived with his daughter Bríghid, his sons Eoin and Columba - and Gracie Mhicky who took care of all of us. We did some madcap things after school and during the evening prep sessions when we were supposed to be studying. An additional memoir would be needed to be written to do justice to this time.

In Dóbhar, Uncle Hugh taught in a two-teacher schoolhouse with his wife Mary, where there was good Irish and instruction was always in Irish. The entrance exam to the Coláistí Ullmhúcháin (Preparatory Schools) gave students from Irish-speaking areas an advantage, because the government of Éamonn de Valera and his party, Fianna Fáil, were committed to the restoration of Irish as the national language.

Subsequent governments welched on this the idea of restoring the language which now gets relegated to one radio station, a television station, and the spontaneous reappearance of the *"Scoil Lán-Gaeilge"*, or the All-Irish school. Strangely, these have been appearing in the suburbs of Dublin, where they seem to provide a happy alternative to the parents who desire them.

Uncle Hugh was an inverate irredentist, and we knew from the map on the schoolhouse wall that the six counties coloured in Orange were *"ours"* and that one day they would all be coloured green like the rest of the counties. In addition to *the map* he had drawn beautiful portraits of Wolfe Tone, Robert Emmett, Pádraig Pearse, and other Irish patriots and hung them on the walls of the schoolhouse.

During his attempt to get elected to the Irish Dáil (or Parliament) on the fervor generated by the foundation of Clann na Poblláchta (Clan of the People), Sean MacBride's new party, Uncle Hugh had us all fired up with the kind of republicanism the party represented.

MacBride was the son of Maud Gonne, the famous subject of W.B. Yeats' unrequited love. Sean MacBride came to our house during the campaign of 1948, and I remember how we followed him into our sitting-room with our mouths wide open. He was a young man then, and spoke fluent French. Subsequent to his political career, he won the Nobel and the Lenin Peace Prizes, the only person in history to win both of these prestigious awards.

Clann na Poblláchta did fairly well in their first election, but Uncle Hugh was not one of those elected. Soon, the fledgling party was riven by dissension over the Noel Browne's mother *and Child Scheme*, which seemed too socialist for the Irish bishops. MacBride's promising party came to a sad ending. Sean MacBride's father, Major John MacBride, was one of the signers of the Declaration of

Independence in 1916, and I believe Uncle Hugh saw in his son the passion for unification of the Republic and the North of Ireland. After the party's demise, Uncle Hugh gave up on political means to secure the return of the North and his loyalties became more pronouncedly republican.

A few years after his death a shameful thing happened, My Aunt Mary was alone in the house with her daughter Bríd on Tuesday, 1 December, 1981. Sometime after 10.00 am a group of Gárdaí - Irish for police - surrounded the house and the outhouses. Then they came in and proceeded to search the house, upstairs and down. One of the Gárdaí stayed with Aunt Mary in the living room, another stayed with Bríd in the kitchen. There were 10 or 12 Gárdaí who took part in this exercise, far too many for two defenseless women. Ostensibly, the Gárdaí were looking for guns. They found none.

Aunt Mary also had nieces, the two Gilliespie sisters, Anne and Eileen, who were arrested by Scotland Yard after the Manchester bombings at the end of 1973. Both served approximately 10 years in prison, and there were many appeals but nothing succeeded. This was probably the flimsy connection to searching my Uncle Hugh's house.

Naturally, Aunt Mary was very upset by the whole incident, and two days later she suffered a major heart attack which caused her to be hospitalized. A second attack followed and she died on Friday night, the 11th of December. Obviously, there is no line connecting dots here – a search and two heart attacks in ten days. A sensible or sensitive squad commander would have known that one or two police would have been enough to search the house. It seemed more like a public relations display for the countryside.

*   *   *   *

Will ye noo come back again
Will ye noo come back again
Many's the heart wid break in twa
Should ye ne'er came back again.

I have always thought that part of my Uncle Hugh's frustration was that he was too intelligent to be teaching in a country school. The breadth of his reading was wide, as was the breadth of his interests. He was involved with the dramatic arts, he could draw and paint, he composed and played music, he had the first windmill in the area to provide his house with electricity. He was handsome by nature and looking out from above his glasses, he was the figure of absolute intellectual authority. In another world, he could have been an Oxford don, or even a film star.

Uncle Hugh was a great believer in the native language and culture, and early in his career became involved with Áine Nic Giolla Bhríde, Conall Ó Fearraí, Tom McBride, Neilly Mulligan, Johnny Sheáin - to name but a few. Together they formed Aisteoirí Ghaoth-Dóbhair, went all over the country garnering award after award for their Irish-language plays. They also founded Aisteoirí Óga Gaoth Dóbhair, which brought schoolchildren into the world of drama.

One of my favourite memories is being part of a small group of schoolchildren who were invited to present a play in the old Abbey Theater in Dublin. The host for this occasion was the Taoiseach's wife, Sinéad, Bean de Valera, who had a keen interest in Irish theater and children's theater. We felt very proud to tread the same boards as the actors in the Synge and O'Casey plays, many of which of are classics to this day. We were awed to be in the famous Green Room where Yeats and Lady Gregory and others gathered so often in the period of Celtic Revival. The old Abbey is gone now, and there is a new theatre in its place, but we who were *from nowhere* – so to speak - had the privilege of rubbing shoulders with the great creative ghosts of yesteryear.

In his later years, Uncle Hugh would inspire and encourage two of his own children, Pádraig and Noël, along with three of his grandchildren, Máire, Cíarán and Pól Brennan to record the Old Irish songs of Donegal. The Brennans were the children of Baba and Leo Brennan who eloped together, and had nine wonderfully gifted children. The first group became known as Clannad (Clann as Dóbhar) and they played to packed houses all over the world, but most especially on the Continent where their music was prized for its originality. They were especially prized in Germany because the Germans loved *die Ur-musik* they played and sang. Anyone who knows Germans knows how highly they value anything that is *Ur*. It means *ancient, original, primordial* in German. Strangely, the word *Úr* means *new* in Irish.

They were to be joined on the road by another gifted member of the Brennans, Eithne Ní Bhraonáin, who later struck out on her own under the name *Enya*. Her musical appeal crosses all boundaries, and her music is prized for it peaceful and contemplative quality. Both she and the members of Clannad have done more for the language than any group that came before them, and they have done it with pride and the knowledge that they were contributing their Irish – and Donegal - treasures to the culture of the world.

Without Uncle Hugh, it is not clear that they would have been there. They aimed high, but they did it with lots of his help in translations - and mostly his important encouragement - that they were doing something very worthwhile.

When he was my teacher, we lived in an Ireland where native Irish speakers were looked upon as backward. Irish was associated with the poorer parts of the country, the congested areas along the West Coast from Donegal to Kerry. These areas were called *congested* because of the density of the population. The origin of the density had its roots in the *factum* that native Irish were displaced by the plantations of James and Mary. After that there came the

Cromwellian push *"to Hell or to Connacht"*, and the massive Ulster plantation after the Williamite wars.

Speaking in Irish took courage. It was almost like standing up for your faith in your own country, which is supposed to be Christian. Looking back on the experience, one can see how well the English had done their work. They knew that to deprive the people of their own culture, the fatal blows had to be to the language, to surnames, place names, and schoolrooms. *To speak the language of home*, as Seumas Deane remarked in a talk at the University of Notre Dame recently, *was also to speak the language of humiliation.*

It was this more than anything else that made the Irish strangers to themselves and to their own land and its ancient culture. Brian Friel captured this loss well in his play, *Translations*. The heartbreak lies in the fact that Ireland had a longer and older culture - especially in its literature and in its oral traditions - than any other modern European country. The government have no will to restore the language - and neither do the people.

*   *   *   *

A covenant with God

"Put me on your heart like a seal
For love is stronger than death;
Stronger than the roar
Of many waters..."

                                    - The Song of Songs

I don't remember our family as being especially religious. We said our prayers by the side of the bed whenever we got up or went to sleep. Those prayers tended to get shorter as we grew older, when the pride of life, that great adolescent wonder, took over from the childlike trust that governed our relationship with God. One could say that a combination of *naivete* - in its best sense - and *immediacy* governed the first relationship; but that does not mean that it lacked a profound insight into the nature of things. Children *can see deeply* into the realities of life.

I call this the great adolescent wonder, respectfully, because for many young people what follows on childhood is sometimes the equivalent of an earthquake in the psychic sense. The second relationship to God is governed by the need of the self to reunderstand itself - due to the onset of puberty *and the need to prove itself*, by standards that are largely set by the peer group. The religion of the father is oftentimes rejected in this period of life. There is less concern with personal truth, more attention given to the opinions of *the crowd*. Therein, sometimes lies a tale of the journey from which some do not come safely home - ever.

Many families in our area had the custom of saying the Family Rosary. We did not, and I suspect that was because we did not have uninterrupted time as a family. Neither did we say grace before meals, because we ate at different times. John and myself became altar boys, so were in the Chapel twice a week. We also accompanied the priest on stations. The custom of *stations* is an old one in Ireland; it was going back to when Mass was said in particular houses in the parish, usually in the areas remote from the Chapel, islands that had no church. This was usually for the benefit of the elderly or physically challenged.

In visits to Annagry Chapel over the years I have observed that altar boys do not change. There is the same jostling for primacy among them, who will carry the processional cross, who will ring the bell and whatever. This infighting makes for pure bedlam, but somehow it sorts itself out; when the sacristy door is opened they prepare angelic faces to march out before the people.

Mother made sure that our family was consecrated to the Sacred Heart, and there was a large picture of Jesus, fairly Catholic looking, with a space below him where the names of my parents, *James and Margaret,* and the seven of us were written in. When Hugh got married, mother added his wife's name, *Sheila,* to the list.

There was another Sacred Heart picture in our bedroom, where it served the additional function of covering a hole in the wall where someone had punched a knot out of the wood. This hole which the Sacred Heart covered was called *the phone.* Whenever fights erupted in the bedroom between John, Tadhg and myself, - and these were nightly occurrences - whoever was being persecuted made straight for the picture, moved it aside, and bellowed into the phone. The sound carried out into the attic above the kitchen, and whoever was below could hear the call for help.

I do not believe that the presence of anyone important in the kitchen was ever enough to keep us from using this means of communication. Neither did the Sacred Heart - who was probably put there to make us behave. This Jesus was a sad, majestic figure with a globe of the world in one hand and a scepter in the other. He looked more lordly and masculine that the one downstairs, at whose feet all our names were inscribed. The *old telephone Jesus* upstairs went with us to the new house, which John built when he came back from Australia in the late fifties.

It was in my dad's room when he died, and it was in Mother's bedroom after that. The devotion must have rubbed off on dad, because he used to pray frequently to the Sacred Heart when he was in pain. Mama used to look at it frequently and wordlessly during the time she was ill. Sometimes, I would ask her, in a half tease and half-serious tone, *"How is the Sacred Heart treating you today, Maggie"*. She would always give the same answer, in a soft voice "I place all my trust in Him". She was never dramatic about this. It was a limpid, candid response, with serene self-assurance.

*   *   *   *

<blockquote>
Whoever at some point
Is seriously wounded by true love
Will never become healthy again
Until she kisses that same mouth
By which she first was wounded...
     - Mechtilde of Magdeburg
</blockquote>

In the Catholic Church, devotion to the Sacred Heart of Jesus has its roots in the middle ages and is associated with Saints Gertrude of Helfta and Mechtilde of Magdeburg, both of whom were women of cultivated intellect and, at the same time, mystics. The devotion was revived in the 17th century by the apparitions of Jesus to St. Margaret Mary Alacoque – the apparitions became known explicitly as those of the Sacred Heart. This devotion that ensued can be described as a focus on the humanity of Jesus and the burning love of His heart, which he wishes to make known to all people. Its spread was fostered by the Society of Jesus which realized that it was one of the best means to counteract Jansenism, a Catholic heresy which can best be described as a Catholic Calvinism.

The spiritual life of France in the seventeenth century was dismal, with the exception of the short-lived beauty of the spirituality of Blaise Pascal, built on the twin poles of reason and the heart. Jansensism effectively crushed the devotional life of the Church with its demand for a rigorous moralism which was not in keeping with Catholic tradition, and which only succeeded in provoking the spirit of the age. The spirit of the age was the Enlightenment.

Ireland had been infected by Jansenism because, in the years before the building of Maynooth in 1795 by the British Government, all of its underground priests would have been educated in the Irish Colleges in France, Spain or the Netherlands. The building of Maynooth as a national seminary was the last gasp of a colonizing force that simply could not control the people, so it turned to the Roman Church with this placebo, which it thought might get them a better grasp on *control* through the spiritual leaders of the country.

It is curious to reflect on how these two influences lived side by side in Irish spirituality for the last few centuries. The devotion to the Sacred Heart was spread in Ireland, as elsewhere, by the Jesuits, and the monthly *Messenger* was read in many homes. The cult of the Sacred Heart was a domesticating force in spirituality, since its emphasis was on prayer in the home. It succeeded in blunting the force of the distant, cold God of Jansenism, while not entirely overcoming it.

Devotion to the Sacred Heart is based on a private revelation, but there is nothing in it that departs from the New Testament, because

Jesus often spoke of his love and compassion for souls. The devotion emphasizes this truth found in the Gospels and in the Pauline and Johannine letters.

There was a side effect to the spread of the devotion in Ireland which was hardly intended by Jesus. It was that his *Messenger of the Sacred Heart* was printed with a brilliant, and suitable, red cover. In days when make-up was only to be seen in magazines and in the films, many's the pale-cheeked girl, or aging spinster lady, who discovered that they could rouge their cheeks by wetting the red cover of the *Messenger* and applying it as carefully as possible for the sake of beauty.

*　*　*　*

> When I find myself in trouble,
> Mother Mary comes to me
> Singing songs of wisdom
> Let it be…

Mother never spoke about her spirituality, and she probably would get flustered if she were asked to describe it. But she betrayed herself in small ways that were not easy to catch. Once, several years before she got ill, she was talking with someone who had just popped into the house to say hello and the person inquired about her health. I was sitting behind her, and heard both of her answers. To the visitor she said, in what is a common Irish response, *"I can't complain"*. Then, in a softer voice for no one in particular to hear, she added: *"I won't complain"*. She could well have said, *"I can't complain, I won't complain, I'll go on"*. But her asceticism was never publicly displayed. And the response came from a constant habit of thanksgiving in which ingratitude had never seemed able to find a beachhead.

After the Easter visit and the experience of hearing mother *"praying in the spirit"*, I called my sister Margaret to test out a hunch that was half-formed in my mind. The hunch was that she had made a covenant with God at some stage in her life, and that might explain this communion with God that gave her such serenity.

Mother probably would not understand the word *covenant,* but she would understand the word *bargain,* or *margadh* as it called in Irish. The only situation in her life where this might have occurred was when Tadhg was young and contracted a severe bronchitis that was going to take him away. mother had often spoken of the night that she and Nurse McCauley, a Lady Dudley nurse for rural people, had sat up with Tadhg, and finally used an old country remedy that worked.

It was strong brown paper with melted butter and paraffin oil on either side. It was clapped tight to his chest, front and back, and then he was bundled up further. Whatever the medical community would say now, it worked and Tadhg got better. My youngest brother was only four at the time, and Maggie always expressed gratitude that he was not lost that night.

Margaret asked her the question. She called me back at Stonehill and said mother was surprised by the question. In any case, she said *no,* she didn't. Margaret said that when she understood the full import of the question, she added in Irish, *"Ni bheadh sin ceart. That would not be right".* The afterthought on the immorality of making bargains with God indicated that she knew clearly that such would demean her relationship to God.

Even though a covenant would not be in the same line as a bargain, I knew enough to back off from this line of questioning. I had run out of hunches, and was, at this point, being confounded by a simpler, more candid mind.

*   *   *   *

The Sounds of War

"May God bless all poor sailors
on the sea tonight,
and send many wrecks
to Ireland's shores..."

- (folk saying)

Mother always described herself as the anchor of our house, and that meant she was usually to be found at home. The only time she had to herself was after she had fed dad and the six boys their Sunday dinner, and then she and Margaret would have their own. Sunday dinner, after late Mass, was the only meal we took together, and it is one of the few things of which I do not have fond memories. It seems as if someone was always getting cuffed or sent away from the table for acting the maggot, or making faces or some other childish thing. It does not say a lot for our family harmony, but such was the case. John says Paddy would grab the whole ration of butter, but Paddy says it was John who started the fights.

Sunday afternoon was *time alone* for mother - and it was not. She usually sat in the kitchen and read the newspaper or did the crossword. Chances are that she would be interrupted several times by children looking to buy candy. Other times she would have visitors. Sometimes she had Denis Néill for the whole afternoon, and him quite inebriated. He would tell her over and over again, *"There are some strange people in this world, Maggie!"* and she would agree with him every time.

Even though we often tried to get her to come with us wherever we were going, she would usually demur. The reason she gave most often was that if someone decided to visit, it would be very inhospitable for them to find the house empty.

When we were young, someone inveigled her into taking a trip to Clydebank, where our Gallagher cousins lived, and to Glasgow where Auntie Mary lived with her husband Eddie. That was in 1939.

A few days after she arrived in Scotland, World War II broke out, and she came scurrying home, along with many other Irish who did not want to be caught up in the war. We teased her afterwards about having caused World War II by leaving home. Truth was, home would never be the same again because of the same war.

*　　*　　*　　*

When the Germans occupied France in July of 1940, the customary shipping routes of England were severely disrupted. The waters of the English Channel were too dangerous for the convoys that Britain depended on for food and war materiel. Ships had to use the northern routes to, and from, the ports of Belfast, Liverpool and the Clyde. The port of London, which was Britain's largest entrepôt, was effectively shut down.

The Allied convoys were in double danger, from the long-range German bombers that operated from France, and the U-boats that lay waiting behind the islands and in the deep bays of Donegal's jagged coastline commanding the west and the north of those maritime lines. British shipping paid a high price. It is estimated that 30,000 British seamen of the Merchant Marine lost their lives in the North Atlantic. Some of the bodies washed ashore in the Rosses and Gweedore, where they are buried in local graveyards at Cruit and Magheragallon.

Death was ecumenical in its catch. There were German and Italian prisoners of war from the wreck of the *Arandora Star*, as well as sailors from Hong Kong, India, the West Indies and other British colonies. On the 18th of October, 1940, the *Derry Journal* reported heavy fire off Bloody Foreland and Gweedore, and a body washed ashore at Gola Island. It was identified as that of Takeshi Uyeda, a sailor of Japanese nationality. On the 23rd of August in the same year, a body fully clothed in naval uniform washed up on Inishmaan Island. The documents on the body identified the corpse as that of Edwin Anderson, born in Sweden, and chief engineer of the M.S. Canton.

There was debris and cargo that washed ashore too, giving rise to the wicked little prayer that coastal dwellers were supposed to say. In any event, beach combing became a fairly profitable pastime for many along the coast. The Derry People advised its readers in November 1940 that seventy gallons of twenty-year-old whiskey landed on the Gweedore coast and was taken into custody by the Gardai and Custom Agents. It added, *"a keen look-out is being kept for further consignments."*

*　*　*　*

Children are not able to connect the dots between cause and effect in something a big as a world war. During the summers, when our Aunt Sarah took us on holiday to our cousins in Meenacladdy, we watched for the convoys that could be seen on the horizon till they disappeared behind Thoraí Island to appear again on its westerly side. We could also hear the sound of guns booming, even when we could not see the ships, and those older than us who could watch at night were able to see fires on the horizon stretching into the Atlantic.

Still, in my memory of this time and especially the summers, I think of John and myself and our cousin Seumas Curran as three kids who were out of a Winslow Homer painting, carefree and timeless, as happy whistling through a blade of grass between our thumbs, or exploring the big tidal pools that lay underneath the cliffs at Laecaite, putting our fingers into sea anemones and feeling their velvety tentacles close in on us, or looking for *goineadars*, small darting fish that had a sting which we both courted and dreaded at the same time.

There was nothing a-bother to us, except exploration, climbing the endless crags and headlands around which the sea broke white, and formed the foamy necklace of our Donegal shores. Later, we became aware that our country was neutral in the war and even though it was reported in the English newspapers that Ireland's neutrality gave the edge to the Germans whose submarines reportedly surfaced to buy fish from the island fishermen, the opposite was true.

The Royal Airforce had a corridor across our county from its bases in Northern Ireland, while the German Luftwaffe had to follow the West Coast, before making a run for the notorious shipping lanes to the north.

Because of this air corridor there were more crashes of British military aircraft in Donegal than in any other part of Ireland. It was also the case that Germans who landed in Ireland were handed over to the British as prisoners of war, while British survivors were quietly repatriated through Northern Ireland. In the early years of the war we were detached, except for the rationing of food, but in the year of 1943 the Second World War was to pay a visit, and its calling card will never be forgotten.

*   *   *   *

"There will be bluebirds over,
The white cliffs of Dover
My darling, just you wait and see.
There will be joy and laughter
And peace ever after
Tomorrow, when the world is free...

It would be hard to explain to any outsider what life was like during the war. Visitors to the area might get an eyeful of mountains, rocks and shore, but they would never suspect how active and intense the social life was during this period. The young virtually danced the war away, almost every evening of week, travelling long distances to dance to favourite bands, coming home in the wee hours of the morning, and sleeping into the afternoon, getting up, eating, and getting ready for the next night's dancing. It was reminiscent of the way the Kuwaiti princes and the entourage of the El-Sabah family danced away the Gulf War in the salons of Cairo.

There was a war, and young people were conscious of it especially in the evening BBC broadcasts, but there was also dating and dumping, smoking and travelling. New friendships were formed, new dance bands were discovered - and the top twenty tunes broadcast from Radio Luxembourg on Sundays were not long in being relayed to the local scene.

The day after a major dance would yield its measure of gossip of who had been going with whom, and who got dumped the night before. One had the impression that the young women were calling the shots when it came to the affairs of the heart. They could afford to be discriminating, because there was an abundance of suitors.

The bands of the time were the Rosses Premier Band, and Ponsonby's Swing Band, Joe Loss with Rose Brennan as vocalist, Victor Sylvester along with a whole bunch of others which did not stay in my memory.

Later, came the Slieve Foy Dance Band which was initially a travelling band, till they came to our area and found it a treasure trove of dancing activity. They decided to settle in Meenaleck and make it their headquarters. My brother Paddy drove them around for a number of years in the old Dodge he bought from Uncle Teague in Gweedore.

During the years of *Clannad's ascendancy* Leo Brennan opened a tavern, also in Meenaleck. *Leo's Tavern*, a well-known locale for musicians from all over Europe, is still there and under the new direction of Leo's son, Bartley Brennan.

In the earlier years Clannad used to spend their summer season there, and they had such a huge following on the Continent that people wanted to see where they came from. Their parents, my cousin Baba Brennan and Leo, had a house directly behind my Uncle Hugh's house, and in their time, both houses were host to many and disparate groupies and music lovers.

* * * *

> Christmas is comin' and the goose is getting fat,
> Please put a penny in the old man's hat.
> If you haven't a penny, a ha'panny will do,
> If you haven't a ha'penny, God bless you.

In the wintertime people played cards and after the autumnal equinox, nightly card games would commence from then till before Christmas. The prize would usually be a bicycle, a turkey or a goose that would wind up as somebody's Christmas dinner. In our house, they played only *twenty-five,* and they occupied the only table in our kitchen.

Consequently, there was no place for anyone else to sit. So, the young folk who were in search of some action - and food - especially around the finals sat on the floor. Later on, there would be tea and bread and jam for everyone and no one would go wanting.

When we, the younger children were around, we had to sit on someone's knee, mess about with the young adults on the floor, or hang about the card table, positioning ourselves between and behind the players so that we could see their respective hands and how well they played them.

It was a great source of pride for us that our Aunt Bridie had a place at the table. Aunt Bridie was a small woman, but as tough-minded as any of the men with whom she played. She and Madgie McFadden were the only two women in the card games, and they contended with seasoned veterans of the game like McDonald, Manus Thimlín, Oweney the Post, Johnny Rodgers, Fr. Michael Carr, our parish priest, Mickey Donie, and Dad, my Uncle James, and lots of other players who came from Annagry, Braade, Bunaman, Mullaghduff, Ranny Thutháil, all the other townlands around. mother got to the table when there was a Big Game, where the contestants played until someone had won, and got all that was left in the kitty.

We all liked the end of the harvesting season because it meant no more herding cows after school. The cattle could go wherever they liked, and the donkeys were let loose too. When nightfall was approaching, and it came early in wintertime, there was a group of us - our John, Hughie and Johnny Hanlon, myself, John Allison and our Tadhg – who used to roam the countryside till we found the donkeys.

The donkeys usually stuck together when they were let out. It was the only freedom they had during the year, and since almost all of them were male, they still did Viagra sorts of things, in the absence of any sex life. Sometime it was difficult to find them, and we were always racing against the dusk of winter evening.

But we rode them home to their owners, and we loved it, because it was the only time we got to ride anything.

The war affected the lives of children in ways that we then attributed to the course of nature. There were outbreaks of scabies, and they were painful. Now we look back and realize that these outbreaks were due to vitamin deficiencies. dad had a remedy that we hated, but for him it was gospel. He would make us cycle to a house above Bunaman, and go to a certain swampy area where bog-asparagus grew.

When we got home with this stuff, he would boil it, and then we had to drink the foulest potion that was ever invented. It was called *"bachrán"*, and dad said it purified the blood. We never contested his medical advice, but whatever its merits, we often had to use another method for scabies that still makes me shudder. It was sitting in a tub of warm water with a scrubbing brush and carbolic soap, and removing the scabs with the brush so that the carbolic soap would get into the wounds.

Things would return to normal when the war ended. I remember quite vividly the first time I saw an orange. It was in 1946 and I was ten years old. A friend of our family, Joe (Lanty) Gallagher was stationed in Gibraltar with the Royal Airforce Force, and he sent us a box with a dozen Seville oranges. Brian Keenan describes in his book, *"An Evil Cradling"*, a terrible period of sensory deprivation in Beirut where he was captive for three years, and the first time he was given an orange instead of the same old, same old, rice and *kibbe*. His words about the orange are ecstatic. We were much the same in our reaction to our box of oranges from Gibraltar, and the whole town gathered in to see them. It was a shared sacrament, but everyone got a taste of the sign of new life.

But this was at war's end. In the early years we were detached, except for the rationing of food, and deprivations of which we were not even aware. Beyond these, the war had other surprises for us. In the year of 1943 World War II was to pay a visit, and its calling card will never be forgotten.

The Fatal Shore

Death, when I am ready, I
Shall come, drifting where I drown...
Falling, or by burning, or by
Sickness, or by striking Down

- T. Kinsella

It would not happened had there not been a war. It wouldn't have happened if there weren't so many young men around. It wouldn't have happened if people obeyed orders. It wouldn't have happened, some said, if a blind beggarman had not laid a curse on the place because he had been badly treated.

But it did happen. On the Monday of May 10,1943, a sea mine floated ashore in between Mullahderg strand and the little village of Ballymanus, about a mile and a half from our home.

It came in a bit south of Annie Shane's house, where Brian Friel now has his summer home, and remained bobbing gently in the water at a place where there was a slight V in the rock formation. The size of the rocks beside it and behind it suggested a strong current coming from behind one of the islands. Those who saw the mine, said it was a brown ball of iron with spikes sticking out at different points on its spheroid surface.

The news of its arrival spread like wildfire, and the boys and young men of Braghaid, Mullaghduff, and Rannyhual rushed down to see it. There would surely have been more had there not been a

Labour meeting in Mullaghduff Hall, and had the news traveled farther afield.

This was not the first mine to come ashore in Donegal, or in other counties of western Ireland. The coast-watching service of the army kept a lookout for them and the ordnance corps did the dismantling. Fisherman James Doogan had spotted the mine earlier in the day, floating towards the shore from the direction of Owey Island at about a mile per hour. This was relatively fast for any floating object, let alone a heavy sea mine that weighed close to 500 lbs.

The mine was a British Mark-14, a so-called "safe" mine. It had a lever that could be in an open or shut position. When the lever was shut, the mine could impact any object - ships, rocks, torpedoes - and nothing would happen. However, the lever had a cable attached in such a way that when it became taut, and pulled the lever open, the mine became activated. Then any one of the spikes could detonate the explosives within.

It was this kind of "safe" mine, broken free from wherever the British had their minefields laid out in the North Atlantic, which finally came to rest in front of a large flat flagstone that afforded a gathering place for those who had come to watch. The time was around 10.00 pm.

May 10, 1943, was cold, according to people whose memories of the day were intense, but it was close enough to the summer solstice that the evening was long and lingering. The sun had gladly gone down, and the moon was not yet visible. The twilight was long enough to create a backscreen of beauty from the islands out fornenst the bay: Owey, and the Stags, Inishfree and Gola. The sea mirrored the sky, sending its bluegreen and opalescent light straight to shore. The stage was set for the dance of death, and the best of the Rosses youth were in the front rows.

The sea never sends in two waves that are alike. You can tell by looking at them that even though they seem so regular, their strength is not equal. In a short time a stronger wave will catch up to a weaker one and their combined strength will cause a swell.

A few of the young men threw a rope around the mine to haul it on to the ledge with the hope of defusing it. As the sea rose on itself, it assisted their efforts to bring the mine onto the ledge of the large flagstone where the young were sitting or standing.

In the stillness a loud wailing was heard coming from far across the sea. It was the cry of *Fóla*, whose name betokens *blood*, one of the three queens of Ireland (along with *Banba* and *Éire*) weeping for her children because the hour of their apocalypse had come. It was 10.53 pm.

Now the mine's cable was presumably caught in the rocks below and swung open the lever that activated the mine. Now each spike tingled with danger and each one had the lethal possibility of being driven into a detonator.

Thus goaded, the mine unleashed its fury, as it flung bodies and limbs into the air, making a charnel house of the ocean as it ran red with the gore and blood of the dead.

No one could ever describe the scene. Those who were left alive with pieces of shrapnel in their bodies could not recall the moment of shock. One of the young lads who died was found without any wounds, a smile still frozen on his face. Others had throats lacerated or limbs blown off. Some were blown to smithereens.

Some of the wounded could only think of running to whatever haven they could. Seventeen died on the spot. John Joe Carson and John Sharkey died later in Letterkenny Hospital. Anthony Rodgers, rushing to the scene to warn the young to come away, was killed in his stride.

The blast, which rocked the twilight, was heard for more than thirty miles around. At the farthest reaches of its sound, people thought it to be thunder, but in the immediate vicinity people seemed to know instinctively what had happened and who might be there.

I was not yet seven but my memory of the moment is acute. I was in a neighbouring house, and when the house shook, the oil lamp, which the owner had just lit a few minutes earlier, came crashing down. Ambrose Dunleavy knew what had happened because his brother, a lieutenant in the Coast Watching Service, had seen the mine when it was near shore at 8.00 p.m. and gave a warning that it should be left alone until it was detonated by the proper authorities.

At that point, all the onlookers were on the banks above the site, still close enough to danger. The lieutenant's warning went unheeded. One woman who recalls the whole scene vividly told me *that it would take an act of God to keep the young men away from the mine.* There was no act of God to refrain them, but only an act of man, waiting to be unleashed - as other young men and boys were on their way to join those already there.

I ran home, but there was no one in our house. mother had left the house, running across the bridge to tell the news to the people on the other side. My brother Jim had already left for the shore to see what he could do. He encountered Hugh Sharkey on the way, with blood on his face. He was one of the lucky ones who would recover from his physical injuries, but who would carry the scars in his memory, and shrapnel in his body, until his death many years later.

The scene at the shore was piteous. Scores of people, young and old arrived at the site, and began combing the seashore and the rocks for loved ones that they thought to be there. The process of identification was almost impossible because of the carnage. Limbs, heads and torsos were everywhere in the water and on the rocky shore. Night fell as this grim task went on. Lorries and cars arrived to convey the bodies to some central location.

No one knows how any kind of order got imposed on the search, the identification which was mostly by bits of clothing that matched, and the conveyal of the remains to the back of one of the lorries. Who was first on the scene, who was carried to nearby houses, who directed this scene from hell, no one can quite remember; but somehow the grisly job got done.

Some of the women went on their knees at the shore, searching the water with both hands and crying at the same time. With black shawls draped across their shoulders, they looked like a Greek chorus trying to influence the gods of war with the voluptuousness of their tears.

They could not realize that what they were doing was futile, but it was their way of making communion with the sea, in total disbelief that it had taken their children away. By midnight, the list of those who were killed or injured: seventeen dead, fifteen injured, and a total of fifty families affected.

One by one the lorries with the bodies spread aboard them began to make their way to Mullaghduff Hall, the only suitable place where a mass wake could be held.

There was to be a farewell dance here in two days time for some of the victims who were going to work as agricultural hands in the fields of Scotland. The streamers of coloured crêpe for the dance were still hanging on the hall ceiling when the bodies began to arrive, the slippery, tinseled stardust still on the polished floor.

The bodies were laid on the floor until the difficult task of identification was complete around 4.00 a.m. The parents and relatives of the dead were admitted in relays and those doing the work had to deal with their grief and still accomplish what they had to do. The remains were subsequently placed in coffins, which lay unmounted on the floor. A piece of cardboard or paper with the name of each of the victims was placed at the head of the coffins.

The people then poured in to take their places beside their loved ones, and their family members and friends came to console them. Many of those who came had brought blessed candles that were in their homes from the previous Candelmas, the second day of February. They held the lit candles in their hands, and the glow cast eerie shadows on the unmounted coffins lined up in rows on the floor.

The prayers began and continued without pause till the break of day. There was no need for leaders here because everyone knew how to lead the Rosary and to take their part in it. mother was there with the older members of our family giving emotional support to the bereaved many of whom were her close friends.

Madgie Shéarlais who lost *Joseph,* Maggie Anna Bheag from Isle of Uist in Scotland, who lost her 14-year old *John.* Dominic Rosie and his wife who lost three sons. They could not understand what God had done to them, nor they to Him, to merit such a grevious cross.

People in the Irish-speaking areas of Ireland are usually very quick in their manner of praying. To an observer, the prayers in Gaelic could seem incantatory, but there were no onlookers or disaffected persons. It was a scene of several villages at prayer simultaneously, and sometimes in shifts – so that those within could break for a respite of fresh air, and those waiting outside would get a chance to enter and join the communal prayer.

People in Donegal always prayed to be spared from "*bás tobann*", a sudden death. It was one of the things most dreaded in their faith, not death itself but the way in which it came.

In another circumstance, one would have been given a small space, even if one's lifeblood gushed out in torrents. There would be time to think a little, say a prayer, think of loved ones - even if it were the thinking of the dream, before the *traüme* of the psychologists became the *trauma* of the physician.

The prayer to be spared a sudden death, after all, is not something new. It has been carried down in the litanies that were recited during the Rogation Days, the Asking Days, during the spring and harvest, when the Church prayed for - or gave thanks for - good crops. In the Litany of the Saints, after the petitions to be spared from all evil and all sin, the one that follows reads in Latin, "a subitanea et improvisa morte, libera nos Domine - from a sudden and unprovided- for death, free us, O Lord".

Flannery O' Connor whose ancestors carried the same faith to Savannah, and later to Milledgville, Georgia, where she lived, has this to say in one of her writings". I have never been anywhere but sick. In a sense sickness is a place, much more instructive than a long trip to Europe, and it's always a place where there's no company, where nobody can follow. Sickness before death is a very appropriate thing, and I think that those who don't have it miss one of God's mercies".

It is interesting to compare the attitudes which different cultures adopt in the face of death. How often, one hears someone recount a death by massive heart attack or something similar, and then the phrase, "That's how I would like to go out. No suffering, no bother"! A premium seems to be placed on the quick exit, the absence of suffering. Yet, one does not hear the same attitudes expressed about sudden death accompanied by violence. One wonders if people are really serious about what they mean when they say these things or whether they really think them through.

In the language more imbued with Christian faith there is no preference for a sudden or pain free death. This is due, in part, to the conviction that the cross is an integral part of life on earth, and that sickness and suffering are part of that mystery. If meaning is to be found in them, it is in the Pauline phrase, that they are a way to make up the sufferings of Christ. In this light, suffering achieves a cosmic meaning. It is redemptive for the life of the world, and for the life of all human kind.

Having said this, none of these beliefs sees suffering as desirable, because in itself it is an evil. Even Jesus sought to avoid the suffering that lay before him, and begged to be spared from it. And conceding the reality of suffering in human life, it is certainly not an excuse to inflict suffering on any man, woman, or beast of burden.

There is a clear desire in the prayer of the early church to be spared from sudden death of any kind. It is because most people need a spatium poenitentiae or a space for repentance. This is to straighten out an individual's relationship with God or with significant others in his or her life, if that be possible.

For myself, these habits of the heart declare the simultaneity of all time in the face of the Eternal. The prayers that ascended like a loud wail from Mullaghduff Hall were intended to pierce the heart of God because the manner of death for so many mothers' sons was, indeed, an evil, and that it had come in evil way.

The faithful were making up the spatium poenitentiae with a firm belief in the communion of saints – an article of the Apostles' Creed - that what someone does of good in this life can be partaken of by others, in love, in another stage of being.

Eternity is not to be thought of as something that is added on to the end of time, our own time or the time of others. Rather, eternity is a reality that is present in every Now, and accessible from every Now. Those who die, said a holy man, go only as far as God, and God is very near.

For us, time is a long succession of befores and afters. From the moment of creation onwards, when time began, until the time of the apocalypse when time will cease, there is an abyss before human life and there will be another abyss after human life, or all life, if it is totally extinguished.

The simultaneity of all this merely says that all creation - and therefore time - is but an instant before God, even though for us it is a procession of days, months, years, centuries, millennia, eras and aeons - and whatever else is used to describe the vastness of this succession. We finally run out of words to describe it, because we cannot even imagine it. The endlessness of the ocean or of the desert, sometimes speak to our imaginations of what this might be, but even they pale before the reality - which is only experienced as discrete moments by those who are alive.

There is another thing that comes to reinforce this idea, and it comes from the testimony of the saints, mystics and non-mystics alike. It is this: many of the spiritual writings of the saints speak of the ability to live in the moment, without thought of a before or after, or without thought of the past and the future.

I found this idea of simultaneity fits nicely with belief in the Communion of Saints as proclaimed in the earliest of the known Christian creeds. I also found a live correlation in a biography of Padre Pio, the Italian stigmatist, who was recently beatified. He habitually recommended prayers for the departed.

To a spiritual daughter, Pio advised, " *Even if your parents are in heaven, we must always pray. If they no longer need prayers, they are applied to other souls". He even recommended prayer for people long dead. He told a friend, " Maybe you don't know that I can pray even now for the happy death of my great-grandfather.... For the Lord, the past doesn't exist, the future doesn't exist. Everything is in a eternal present. Those prayers had already been taken into account. And so I repeat that even now I can pray for the happy death of my great-grandfather".*

The days that followed the mine disaster were filled with disbelief that this could, or did, happen. They were also filled with prayer which continued for one month in Mullaghduff Hall. Half of the bodies were removed to Kincasslagh Church, the other half to Annagry Church.

We were not allowed to go near Mullaghduff Hall during the wake, not so much from a desire to protect us, as a way of leaving as much space for the bereaved and their dead. But no one could protect us from seeing the procession that wound its way from the Hall, down our brae and across to our parish Church.

There were no counselors in those days to help people deal with their grief, their anger with God who permitted this to happen, and the authorities who should have taken faster action. The doctors and the local clergy, including those who had served in these parishes, before the disaster, did their best to comfort the people, even though they were also shattered by the experience.

We were lucky that the priests in the several parishes of the Rosses and Gweedore, Kincasslagh and Dungloe were excellent men in their holiness and integrity, high in the respect of the people, and humble in themselves. Their work was not easy, but they gave the experience of evil as consolatory a face as it could have under the circumstances. But it wasn't easy.

It is never easy. Here's how Augustinian Father Pádraig Daly expresses it in his poem *Ministers:*

It is we who are kicked for your failures;

When pain lasts across the night,
When people gatherly helplessly around a bed,
When grief exhausts the heart,
It is we who must bear the anger.

When love fails,
When friends are gone,
When words are rubble
When eyes cannot lift to see the sun,
People ask us to explain; and we are dumb.

When rage against you is a fierce sea
We are the first rocks on the shore.

*   *   *   *

Last year, Pat Gallagher, the son of one of the victims headed up
an effort to put a stone monument above the place where the mine
came in. It is made from ordinary fieldstone in the shape of a cairn,
and it has a simple plaque commemorating the event. Hardly
anyone went there after the disaster and it is still a lonely place. It
is called Rann na gCaorach (the Share of the Sheep). His mother
was putting Pat and his brother to bed when she heard the
explosion, never even thinking where her husband was. When she
reached the place in the company of other women, a priest whom
she knew put his arms around her and told her what had happened.
He asked her not to go farther to the scene of death. And she did
not. *"I lived a pretty lonely life after that"*, she said without any trace of
self-pity, *"I never went out much since then"*. By itself, her simple tone
of voice acknowledged that death left a long shadow in its wake.

*   *   *   *

.... Time was when the little toy dog was new,
And the soldier was passing fair
But that was the time when little Boy Blue
Kissed them and put them there.

Mullaghduff Hall still stands, a mute and rusted witness to all that happened. Few ever danced there again. When we had to pass by it, especially if we were alone and it was night, we would avert our eyes from the hall for fear that we might see something frightening. We all knew that the blood of the victims had seeped out of the coffins and had gathered in a pool at the lower end of the hall.

It was not without reason that Mullaghduff Hall became a place to be avoided. Some strange things had happened there before the mine, as if it were an omen of what would happen. One night a couple who were well-known to me took refuge in the hall one night during their courtship... The future husband played in the band that performed there regularly. He was the only one who had a key. There was another entrance, a back entrance, to the hall, but that was shut and locked. No one ever used it.

A few minutes after their entrance, the two heard a series of loud noises coming from the direction of the stage. It was described by one of them as a loud shuffling noise that was not normally associated with anything they knew.

As the noise grew louder, then stopped, they became aware of a presence that was approaching them, until it was almost upon them. They grew faint as the uncanny presence approached them, and clung to each other for support. The presence had now become the sound of heavy, labored breathing, too loud to be human. It was almost upon them. They rose to make for the door, and what would be a matter of seconds became at least ten minutes because their legs were so weakened with fright, they would hardly carry them.

Finally outside, they walked home as rapidly as they could. The man was going to find a friend of his, and return with a flashlight to see if they could discover the source of terror. His wife later told me that he had come to the conclusion that it wasn't anything he could find, and that he did not want to have another encounter with the uncanny presence.

His wife told this to no one, but with the passing of time she became willing to talk about it. There was no doubt in her mind that it was the presence of someone who was, as she put it, *"not at rest"*. She was not the only one who felt this way about Mullaghduff Hall. Many people had vibes of the unspeakable as they passed up or down the road in front of it. I passed it many times myself on my bike, and if it was dark, I would whistle my way past it, with my eyes turned to the other side of the road.

* * * *

Memories and cherry blossoms

'the soul needs to be honored with a new dress woven from green and blue things and arguments that cannot be proven' - P. Kavanagh

About ten years before her death, mother had a heart attack and nearly died. She did not know she was having a heart attack because she had never been seriously ill before, and she had no analogous knowledge that would permit her to guess what was happening to her.

She described the heart attack as a pain that felt as if her gullet was on fire. It prompted her to take some baking soda because she diagnosed her pain as severe heartburn. When she was finally diagnosed properly, she had to go to the hospital in Letterkenny for treatment. She did not like hospitals and made it clear to us that if anything like this happened again, she would prefer to stay at home, and, as she put it, *"take her chances"*.

Mother was 82 at the time. The doctor who treated her told us that the problem was simply clogged arteries, and that at her age, he would not consider doing an intervention. He added that surgeons in the United States would not hesitate to do a by-pass, but that in Ireland it was not to be recommended. Neither myself, nor any members of the family demurred. In any case, the proposition would never be made to mother.

I went home when I heard she was ill and that it was serious. The weather was cold and rainy beyond compare, and as I drove from Calhame to Letterkenny and back for ten days or so, the journey seemed longer than the thirty miles it was because of the downpour.

The glen that opens beyond Errigal Mountain was filled with water gushing down the side of the heather-clad hills. There was water running up the mountain and down the mountain - gorging, spouting out of the mountainside, flowing to the north in search of escape. Even the road itself became a stream because it ran downhill all the way to Gartan. I often thought it was a shame that so much fresh water should go to loss, because the Donegal Mountains rarely lacked for irrigation. If the road to Letterkenny were a Sahara or the Sahel, it could surely slake its parched dryness with such a watery bounty.

Mother almost died one night while she was in the hospital. We knew something was wrong when the nurses asked us to leave and pulled the curtains around her bed. Medical folk in Ireland are generally parsimonious with information – and that is a mild judgement - but we found out somehow that her blood pressure had dropped precipitously, and that they almost lost her. I think they changed the medication she was taking and her blood pressure plunged in response to it.

Anyway, she got well, changed to a diet with less cholesterol, and took her medication regularly, rested longer in the morning and went to bed at midnight - unless there were visitors, or a snooker championship on television in which one of her favourites was playing.

This entire new regimen took place under the watchful eye of my sister Margaret. Crucial to the new regimen was mother's staying in bed until noontime. Whenever I went home to visit afterwards,

Margaret would urge me to stay in bed until noontime, too, because, she said, if mother knew that I was up, she would get restless and feel that she had to be up as well, to see that I was being properly treated and fed. It did not take much urging to make me fall in with this plan because my definition of luxury is the ability to sleep late mornings, as long as I got the daily newspapers when they arrived.

Mother observed this new life style without complaint. She had a glass of warm water when she woke up around eight-thirty, and this was followed by a bowl of thin porridge with milk. The warm water, slowly sipped, was a recipe she inherited from her father. He had taught his children that this was the most healthful thing they could do after rising. The reason was that it relaxed the esophagus, the stomach and bowel, and brought the bodily corporation to attention in the most gentle of ways.

Some years after this, mother mentioned to me in passing that she was glad she did not die at the time of the heart attack. She did not do this to elicit any reaction from me, but to give herself a chance to make another observation. *"The memories"*, she said, *"were too good"*. I must have said something in return but I do not recall that now. But I never forgot the reason she gave for being glad she did not die, because it was one of those comments that said a lot about the way she lived her life.

> O, many miles I've traveled and
> a million sights I've seen; and I'm
> Ready for the glory now to be.
> But I wonder, oh yes, I wonder
> Will the angels way up yonder,
> Will the angels play their harps for me.

Hirokazu Kore-eda, the Japanese film director, made a movie last year called *After Life*. It is set in a drab office building where a group of caseworkers seem to follow the needs of their weekly load of clients. After a while it becomes clear that these are not social workers, but people who are doing serious and very special work and their clients are of varying age and background - who have just died.

One by one the living-dead are assigned to caseworkers and told that they have three days to make a choice of a particular memory to take with them into the next world. When they have chosen, the staff will do its best to make sure that they have individual home movies to take with them into eternity.

A gentle, decrepit old woman has fondest memories of cherry blossoms, an aviator chooses the moments of his flying through the clouds and so on. Some refuse to make a choice - even though their entire life was put on playback for them, as often as they needed a fresh review.

If one refuses to choose, one has to stay in limbo, because that is exactly where the social workers are, helping the newly dead to prepare a happy memory that will grant them entrance into the world beyond. In a sense, the memory movies are a way of making the dead pronounce life *good* before they move them on to a better life.

While watching the film, one of the things that occurred to me, was that mother might have to stay in limbo a long time, not because she did not have a good memory to be videotaped, but that she had too many of them. She would be very good at convincing others of the goodness of their memories, too. She could gently drill the cynicism or bitterness out of a person's life without his being aware of it. Her spirit of joy was a contagion.

Memories are not automatic. They arise from the way the mind lovingly caresses the past, not changing its reality, but suffusing it with a soft loving glow; even changing the dross of experience, and the drabness of everyday life, into something that is golden.

Mother had whatever alchemy it took to do this, and not as a one-time experience. I think her constant prayer, especially her prayer of thanksgiving, made her heart grateful for life and for all that happened in it. This included suffering too.

If there is anything fundamental to what can be said of her, it is that she never ran away from her crosses, as many of us do, but rather accepted them willingly as part of her mystery of redemption. She learned to find that in her grasp she had, instead, a renewed life in place of something that could have crushed her down. She was what Flannery O'Connor would call a *muscular Christian,* a term not easily grasped by those who are not muscular.

*   *   *   *

Monks, Prostitutes, and Saving Love

Vitium impotens, Virtus vocatur
Impotent vice is called virtue
                                        - Seneca

I recall a visiting lecturer in philosophy who came to address the students at Stonehill in the heady days of anti-war protests, free speech, Angela Davis, Herbert Marcuse, Black Panthers, Woodstock, pot-smoking and free love. The lecturer did not come to speak about the bedlam that existed in the United States, but came to speak about the nature of love.

He carefully delineated all the needs of the human being; for food and drink, for rest and activity, for achievement, for sex, for sleep, for dreams, for a good name, and so on. He also listed at the end, *the need to be loved.* He then said that *to love* was not a need, and should not be thought of, or analyzed in this way. The students almost went wild with protest at what he said. On the face of it, it was a fairly innocuous statement, but we were submerged in a therapeutic culture, where everything is defined as *a need* - and then *a right.* We have not yet emerged from this therapeutic culture, which despite its healing name has the capacity to make social life and culture a bit more than putrid.

The reason why *to love* cannot be a need is, simply that love is an overflow from another person, a giving that does not have to be given, a going out of oneself towards the other, even a gift of oneself to the other. It is not *a need*, it is not an *investment* in the other, it is not a *quid pro quo.* These latter descriptions denigrate love, and even argue against the possibility of altruism in human beings. Surely, the cynic thinks, at the bottom of the heap of gold, some mean motive will be unearthed to make it *not real.*

Real human love will have an effect, and one of those effects will be its *the saving character.* We are accustomed to thinking of the divine love of Christ as being redemptive, but sometimes we are not sure about who is being redeemed and from what - and to what end. Most people have a rough idea.

We can ask the same question about human love. Does it, in effect, have a saving character too? This question became important to me and to several of my brothers, when we were able to share our experience of having been "*saved*" from the consequences of our own acts, and that somehow we traced this to Maggie - who did not intervene directly in our affairs, but did pray (we knew) that *we might come safely home* out of the contagion of evil which we courted. Furthermore, she also prayed that we would find a way out of *the suffering* that sin causes. This conclusion led me to seek some passages in literature where the power of saving *love* is portrayed and more easily understood.

In his novel, *The Brothers Karamazov,* the Russian writer Dostoyevsky creates a rich panoply of characters who mirror conflicting and confusing ideas about God, mankind, the possibility of nihilism, socialist revolution, the nature of the ideal state; the ideal Orthodox Church of *sobornost;* love, lust, greed, pride and sensuality - in short, just about everything in the human condition. Part of Dostoyevsky's genius is that he can portray the entire spectrum of *belief and unbelief, sin and grace,* in a novel that works on several levels.

One of the most sympathetic characters in the book is that of Alexei, whose pet name is Alyosha. He is an improbable antagonist, but he is the one who is moving through the whole story. He has entered the monastery as part of his personal struggle to escape from *darkness into light.* It is an understatement to say that there is not a great deal of light in his family. There are two other brothers in the family, Ivan and Dmitri. Neither of them is a role model, nor did they fall far from the tree.

Their father Fyodor is notorious for spending money on women and drink - usually money that he has knocked out of other people. There is nothing secret about his life or about his opinions. He believes that sin is sweet, that everyone lives in it; and what others do on the sly, he does openly. He scoffs at Alyosha's idea of Paradise, and believes that he will not wake up after his death.

Strange as it may seem, Alyosha goes to his father to ask his blessing as he leaves his home for the monastery. The old man launches into a fairly cynical musing on his son's venture, but at the same time his affection for Alyosha is enough to pierce his heart. Alyosha is the only one who has never condemned his behavior. While he was with his father, *he saw every thing and said nothing.* He even had a natural devotion to the old man. His father is keenly aware of his son's simple nature and of the non-judgemental quality of his outlook on the behaviour of others. He gives his improbable blessing to his improbable son.

In the monastery, Alyosha is attracted to the elder, Zosima, who has a reputation for holiness, even though he, too, had led a fairly rough and hoe-down life in his youth. Alyosha's love and respect for his spiritual mentor is so strong that it makes his faith a bit naïve. When Zosima dies, Alyosha expects his body to remain incorrupt. Instead, it begins to decay prematurely - and this becomes the topic of conversation everywhere, because everyone has noticed the smell emanating from the body in the monastery chapel where Zosima is being waked.

This is traumatic for Alyosha's faith. He expected a higher judgement for his beloved spiritual father who is now being jeered at by a frivolous crowd, among them monks who were jealous of Zosima's reputation for holiness. Alyosha is beset with questions. Why did Zosima have to decay so prematurely? Why has Providence taken cover at such a crucial moment?

Sensing that Alyosha may be at the point of rebellion against God, a shady character named Rakitin approaches him. Like many of the sons of the lower clergy, Rakitin is the son of a priest and a nihilist. Rakitin also has designs on Alyosha. He has been promised money by the beautiful Grushenka who wants to tear the cassock off the monk. Ratikin is also interested in bringing Alyosha down, and destroying his innocence – a classic example of how innocence must be destroyed by those to whom it has become a reproach.

Ratikin approaches Alyhosha and asks him if he is in rebellion against God because Zosima has begun to stink. Alyosha is initially unresponsive because he is irritated by the questions. *Finally he says that he accepts God but not his creation.* These words, curiously, are those of his brother Ivan from an earlier conversation the brothers had on the God-question.

Then the depressed Alyosha takes sausage and vodka from Ratikin and consents to go with him to Grushenka. Alyosha tells Rakitin that because he lost his treasure - his spiritual father - he felt evil and wanted to go to Grushenka to find someone wicked.

Grushenka had to be the hottest show in town because she is not only his father's whore, but also his brother Dmitri's. She has lusted after Alyosha partially because she wanted to bring his innocence to heel.

Grushenka is surprised to see Alyosha, and told him she doubted he would ever come to see her. She asked him why he was depressed and whether he was afraid of her. She then got on his knee and put her arm around him to cheer him up. But Alyosha does not move or tell her to get off. *This is a moment of spiritual crisis for both of them.* He came not caring what happened, but he sees goodness in Grushenka. In turn, his kindness has an effect on her and moves her to confess.

She tells him she loves him with all her soul, even though at times she had sly designs on him. At other times, she looked on him as her conscience and thought he must despise her.

He answers no, that he found in her a true sister and a loving heart. He tells her she has raised his soul from the depths.

Alyosha's experience here seems to underline the idea that *any love which is expanding and intensifying is being purified, and cannot in the end prove dangerous.* As for Grushenka, everything tumbles out of her, and *she tells him that she has believed all her life that someone would really love her and not with a shameful love.* In a way, she is like the woman who approached Jesus at a banquet, washed his feet with her tears and dried them with her hair. She knows somehow that this person will not turn her away because she is a prostitute, nor will he use her with the only kind of shameful love she has known until now. Grushenka senses the same thing in Alyosha.

What I have written here in sketchy fashion is to indicate that Dostoyevsky regards the interaction between Alyosha and Grushenka as a case of moral regeneration in which one person restores another. The effect of Alyosha's selfless love on Grushenka is no less potent than the effect she has on him.

In another place, after having a dream of Zosima in heaven, *Alyosha throws himself upon the earth, kisses it, sobs, and promises to love it forever.* Alyosha is putting aside the scorn his idealistic faith had for the world of matter, to which his beloved Zosima is returned.

Alyosha's scorn for the stuff of which we are made is, indirectly, a scorn for people. He had to learn more clearly that human beings are not pure spirits, that the world of flesh is the world which Christ came to inhabit, and that Christian faith is more incarnational than his too spiritual gnostic view.

The context indicates that Grushenka has given him back his faith in mankind, and its redeemability. Indirectly, he is also given back the faith he had in God, the faith that had been severely shaken by the stumbling-block of Zosima's stinking and decomposing body.

*   *   *   *

Beauty is momentary in the mind -
The fitful tracing of a portal;
But in the flesh it is immortal.
The body dies; the body's beauty lives.
- Wallace Stevens

There is probably no other novel where *the saving power of human love* is treated as fully and delicately as in *The Brothers Karamazov*. I use it as a powerful backdrop for some observations on the love we experienced from our mother.

It is not only the Alyosha of the novel who has difficulty with his faith in the face of the rotting body. *We all do.* We all have the same difficulty when we are faced with the decline of the mental and physical powers of our loved ones. Many in our time have the same traumatic experience with a parent's Alzheimer's as Alyosha had with the decaying Zosima.

The question of God's fairness arises. Is there not a higher justice for those whom we love? And where is God's providence hiding itself at times of loss and grief. One of my closest friends in the College refers to this latter as *the moral silence of the universe,* mute in the face of human tragedy. His view would be an antithesis to Ivan's opinion on the meaning of life, for he sees the universe as beautiful, but not the morally silent *Whatever* that lies (or doesn't lie) behind it.

* * * *

There are no easy answers to these questions, and there should be no attempt at glib answers from those who believe. In my own opinion, the believer is more likely to encounter stumbling-blocks than the atheist, the agnostic or the strictly secular humanist.

The fact remains that God and his creation *are not easily reconciled.* God is not easily reconciled with nature *"red in tooth and claw"*. God is not easily reconciled with the so-called *"acts of God"*, the floods, earthquakes, the droughts – the human tragedies which we now see so often on our television screens. God is not easily reconciled with *the wars, the ethnic cleansings,* with Rwanda and Burundi - the pure hatred of people who even share the same patrimony of faith. God is not easily reconciled with a Lebanon or a Kosovo which permit the mutual massacres of those who share the same Abrahamic faith. God is not easily reconciles oftentimes with ourselves and our impulses.

As an old Italian spiritual master says about the difficulty of union with God, "È *difficile impastarsi con Dio"* / *"It is difficult to make pasta of one's self and God".* He is referring to the task of rolling out the sheet of pasta, which is metaphor for intimate union with God.

* * * *

No one knows where Maggie's love affair began. In fact, she may not have known herself. It may have been a steady deepening of her prayer, an initial gift of contemplation; it may have been an epiphany as simple as that of Brother Lawrence. His story is well known to many people, but I will repeat it here.

Lawrence says that at the age of eighteen God had done him a singular favour in his conversion:

"That in the winter, seeing a tree stripped of its leaves, and considering that within a little time the leaves would be renewed, and after that the flowers and fruit appear, he received a high view of providence and the power of God, which has never since been effaced from his soul."

That this view had perfectly set him loose from the world, and kindled within him such a love of God that he could not tell whether it had increased during the more than forty years he had lived since.

The epiphany of Lawrence involved a natural thing, and he was allowed to see - in analogous fashion - something like it in the realm of grace. His simple account has a nice ring to it, and his observation that *"it enkindled in him such a love for God that he could not tell whether it had increased during the more than forty years he had lived since"* – this is perfectly in tune with more famous mystics who would say exactly the same thing and, more honestly, that sometimes they were confused about whether they loved God at all.

The late Cardinal Hume of Westminster says somewhere that *God could make you a saint at any time, but you would not know it.* This seems like a strange statement, but it one reflects on it, one will see the truth in it: that among saints, the greater sense of the holiness of God, the greater the sense of their own nothingness and sinfulness.

This is as true of Isaiah and Jeremiah as it is of Francis of Assisi, Theresa of Àvila, John of the Cross, Catherine of Siena, Lady Julian of Norwich - even Abraham, the father of all believers. When one follows a saint, mystic or not, through the times of comfort and of trial, one finds them at times very aware of the holiness of God, at other times confused about whether or not they are on a journey to a chimera.

Like the simple acts of Alyosha that resulted in the moral regeneration of others, several of us in our family - and some outside the family - could attest to similar instances of moral regeneration or release from suffering that were somehow traceable to Maggie. We did not know how or when - we just knew it.

It should be noted that moral regeneration, when it occurs, *has no touch of the miraculous about it* - as people commonly understand the word: *a suspension of the laws of nature*. It is more of *a push, a prod, a waking-up*, maybe even a realization that we are in a rut, at a dead end, going nowhere, and yet sensing that there has to be a better way, because we see this in the lives of others.

Indeed, the individual may experience a greater intensity of suffering or a feeling of greater bondage in the condition that has him or her captive. *But something new has been born.*

The other thing that becomes clear to the recipient of grace is that a new set of moral habits is not provided immediately with the experience of moral regeneration. You may have scales fall from your eyes, or you may have your head turned around from the direction it is facing. That is the grace - a gentle push, a shove, a slow dawning.

The rest is a not sheer plòd, but it will involve some of that. This may be an attempt to cultivate virtues that have not been cultivated in years. *There is happiness at the glimpse of freedom, there is dismay at all the things one will have to forego.* The will is there, but it may have to call up some spiritual muscles that are flabby because they have not been used either for a long time - or ever.

Frequent prayer - even though brief - will be essential. You don't have to go it on your own, and you cannot go it on your own. Going your own way may be what got you there in the first place.

There is a reality called *grace* that is too widespread to be ignored in the lives of ordinary people, especially in the lives of those who belong to the greatest social movement in the history of the last century, the subterranean movement called Alcoholics Anonymous. Their creed has spread to other compulsions: gambling, narcotics, eating disorders, child or spousal abuse, violence. It requires a recognition of a Higher Power, solidarity with others who are looking for liberation, along with an attempt to live in the moment.

*   *   *   *

Setting the stage for a new period in Mother's life was that, beginning in 1953, my oldest brother Jim left for London, Pat left for Toronto, I left for Boston, and John left for Sydney and the Snowy Mountains. Tadhg, the youngest, left for Galway. The only ones left at home were dad, Hugh, Margaret and Maggie.

I have mentioned before that mother went as far in the National School as she could go. That was until age 14, in the seventh class. She was good at composition and had beautiful handwriting. She would have to deploy both for our sakes for the rest of her life. And she did.

Wherever we were, we could look to her for a letter each week, or each second week. These were composed and written for each individual, and they would contain the news that she thought would interest her recipient. She sent hundreds of these letters to those of us who were in the family's Diaspora. They were long letters, sometimes fourteen or fifteen pages long.

We knew her heart was a lonely hunter, and she always stayed with the chase, whether she was acknowledged or not. It was not just the thoughtfulness, or even the news, but there was always a hope expressed that we were well, and a prayer of protection to keep us safe.

And all this was expressed in love. Her faithfulness never knew risks we took, nor the contagion of evil which we sometimes courted like old Fyodor who told his son Alyosha that sin was sweet and that most people lived in it.

Mother seemed to have appropriated an insight which is nicely described in a small collection of letters written to famous people like Shakespeare, Dickens, Pinocchio, and others by *John Paul I, Albino Luciani*, who was Pope for thirty-three days. The last letter in the book Illustrissimi is addressed to Jesus, and in it the Pope says, *"You really seem - this is my impression - to be more concerned with the sufferings that sin produces in the sinners that with the offense against God"*.

This is a fairly bold statement, but it is consistent with the attitude of Jesus towards sinners, and apart from the sin against the Holy Spirit, which cannot be forgiven, it bears our own experience that our sin will eventually cause only ourselves or others to suffer. God is not diminished by human evil because it is No-thing, but rather the absence of something that should be there. We do not blame a rock for lacking compassion, but it should be present in a human being. Its absence, in the case of the human, is evil.

St. Augustine who had plenty of experience with sin when he was Manichean, *was the first to point out that evil, and therefore sin, are privative* - that they are an absence of being where it should be, as compassion, for example, should be part of being human.

Lady Julian of Norwich who was married, had children, was widowed would probably not be able to understand Augustine's definition, but in simpler language she would say the same thing. In one of her shewings or visions she has an explanation in her simple clear language:

I did not see sin.
For I believe it has no substance or manner of being,
but is only known by the pain it causes. (27)

These remarks about evil being no-thing and privative are not to be construed that we should not be concerned about it. It always inheres in a subject, whether that subject be human or angelic, or whatever.

We generally do not impute sin to rocks, scorpions or tigers. But even in its Hebrew and Greek version, too far from our linguistic ken, the word *sin* means *"missing the mark"*. In Greek it carries the *alpha privative*, indicating it is something *missing,* something not there, some action that missed its goal.

*　　*　　*　　*

You know I heard about people like me,
But I never made the connection...
They take one road to set them free,
And find they've gone the wrong direction.

Clare Cotton is the head of the Association of Independent Colleges and Universities in Massachusetts. He is a graduate of Randolph–Macon College in Georgia. His father was a man of the cloth, and I think some of his eloquence must have rubbed off on his son.

Every so often he says to me, *"You know the single greatest thing in Roman Catholicism was that thing you guys passed at the Council of Trent – the bit about the validity of the sacrament not being dependent on the worthiness of the minister"*.

Recently, I asked Clare how he even knew about such a decree from the great Council which was brought on by the Reformation, and what the occasion was for his discussing it, as he obviously had.

He said he was being interviewed by the news media about Watergate and whether or not Nixon had debased the presidency. He said he did not think so, because there was a distinction to be made between the office and the person who held it. Then, he said to me, *"I remembered this piece from one of my courses in college, and I quoted it for the journalist so that he would understand the point I was making"*. The journalist must have been surprised at Clare Cotton's erudition to go so deep in the hole for this clunker of an analogy.

But *it is true* that the Council of Trent felt obliged to make this declaration about the validity of the sacraments not depending on the worthiness of the minister. The ministers at the time were not the most moral creatures, and Luther tried to protect the faithful by saying that the efficacy of the sacrament depended only on the faith of the recipient.

The Council of Trent struck back by two canons. *One said the sacrament was conferred by the performance of the rite itself (ex opere operato) and to emphasise it further, another canon declared that even a minister in the state of mortal sin, as long as he observes all the essentials that belong to the performing and conferring of the sacrament, does so validly.* The Council obviously does not condone the latter kind of behaviour, but wants to protect the faithful by declaring that the moral worthiness of the minister does not affect the sacrament.

*   *   *   *

The Tridentine teaching on the validity of sacraments not depending on the morality of the minister is probably best described in Graham Greene's novel, *"The Power and the Glory"* through its protagonist, *"the whisky priest"*, who is hunted down in the Mexican persecutions at the beginning of this century. The priest knows he is the only one left in the country "who can put God into the mouths of people", and it is this which keeps him going in the formidable chase in which he is the quarry and the lieutenant is the hunter.

It is also found, to a lesser extent, in *"The Diary of a County Priest"* by Georges Bernanos, where the young Curé expires in the apartment of his friend who is a laicized priest. He writes a letter to the Curé's *anam chara*, L'Abbé de Torcy, saying that he had expressed regrets about not being able to give his the Last Rites, because he had abandoned his priesthood. He noted that the the Curé clasped his hands and said in an almost inaudible voice", *What matter?* Tout est grâce! or *Grace is everywhere!*

Flannery O'Connor is another novelist who is very much insistent on the ontological reality of sacraments. There is a wonderfully wicked passage in her letter, collected in *A Habit of Being*, that illustrates her point. Here she is writing to a friend who is working on a short story:

I was once, five or six years ago, taken by some friends to have dinner with Mary McCarthy and her husband, Mr. Broadwater. (She just wrote that book, *A Charmed Life*.) She departed the Church at the age of 15 and is a Big Intellectual.

We went at eight and at one, I hadn't opened my mouth once, there being nothing for me in such company to say. The people who took me were Robert Lowell and his now wife, Elizabeth Hardwick. Having me there was like having a dog present who had been trained to say a few words but overcome with inadequacy had forgotten them. Well, toward morning the conversation turned on the Eucharist, which I, being the Catholic present, was obviously supposed to defend. Mrs. Broadwater said that when she was a child and received the Host, she thought of it as the Holy Ghost, He being the *"most portable"* person of the Trinity; now she thought of it as a symbol and implied that it was a pretty good one. I then said, in a very shaky voice, *'Well, if it's a symbol, to hell with it'.* That was all the defense that I was capable of, but I realize now that this is all I will ever be able to say about it, outside of a story, except that it is the center of existence for me; all the rest of life is expendable.

This is pretty strong stuff, but it indicates that Flannery O'Connor would accept no explanation of the Eucharist, except the one that *it is really and truly the Body and Blood of Christ.* Her understanding of the Eucharist is *ontological* - not magical, not symbolic, not phenomenological, not anything else - just sacramental and, therefore, *really real.*

There are not many examples in literature of the sacraments as ontological because in the century gone by, the teaching of the Church developed other aspects of the Eucharist and Holy Orders and, for that matter, of nearly all the sacraments. But this will do for the present time, and I bring them up only for one reason.

*   *   *   *

Maggie was in the ontological school. It was not that she wasn't a realist, because in the course of her lifetime she had known many priests, secular and religious. They ranged all the way from the holy and scrupulous - to the folksy and hip. She knew those who battled with their demons, and those who did not seem to have to do that. At the end of the day, priests were all the same to Maggie and she would not join in any discussion of criticism or derogatory gossip, even when I tried to lead her on.

But that was Maggie, and she was not kidding. Her life was centered on Christ, the Great Sacrament of God, on the Mass which she attended daily after we had all left home. She was such a reliable presence, that the parish priest gave her the key to open the Church door each morning. Mostly she joined a group of friends who went by bus, but during Lent, they walked the mile and a half, come hail or windy weather. Maggie seemed to me to be one of those people who *needed* the Eucharist for her nourishment, and for her it was not one of those pieties which people practice to feel fuzzy good. Because of its source it generated the love that made things *come to be* in her own life and in ours.

I took all of Maggie's old prayerbooks with me before I left home. They are so tattered that I had to put an elastic band around them because the binding had worn away, and the pages were coming loose. These were the pages she used for about three hours every morning before she got up. They are sprinkled with prayer leaflets of her favourites saints, and the memorial cards of her friends. They are filled with prayers of trust and confidence in God - and more trust. On the inside of one book, all the birthdays of the children - to the third generation - are written down.

* * * *

Black October

There are three swallow's nests in the rafters above me
And the first clutches are already flying.
Spread this news; tell all if you love me
You who knew that when sick I was never dying'.

- Patrick Kavanagh

The new from home is not good. I have to go to the Midwest today, October 3, to attend the inauguration of the new president at St. Mary's in South Bend. I find myself reluctant to go - for fear I may have to break my journey and come straight back home for prepare for the journey to Donegal. For the past two weeks, mother has been refusing to take anything, even water.

I asked my friend Joy about my mother's refusal to eat or drink. Joy is an emergency-room doctor and seems to know everything about sickness and suffering. Joy says it is easily explainable. The loss of potassium will cause mental confusion, and the loss of sodium will make the muscles weak. When a person is in that state, they will refuse to eat, because they don't know what they are doing.

When I explained about our being in the countryside, she suggested that my mother be given sips of Gatorade. Joy is originally from Burma and she understands the plight of country people who don't have the same array of medical techniques available here. When I mentioned to her that we did not want to use any extraordinary means to keep mother alive, she said softly, *"You can never have a parent long enough".* I can see now how her own reverence for her parents comes from her Buddhist faith. It touches me deeply that at certain times we are all the same. Hossein, my close friend who is Muslim, passed along a message from Marion O'Sullivan in the Dean's office that perhaps someone in the family should let my mother know it was *okay to let go*. Coming from Marion, Hossein probably thought this was a time-hallowed Catholic idea. I think its origin is very modern, maybe in the *Hospice* movement, or in the new *Death and Dying* lore.

When I told my brother Hugh about Marion's message, he looked up from his crossword and said that if someone told him it was okay to let go, he would understand he was being abandoned. The idea hit the dust with that observation.

The inauguration of the new president of St. Mary's went off well. The campus is across the Dixie Highway from the University of Notre Dame. Both campuses are places of great beauty, most of the buildings modern Gothic in Indiana limestone. I could not help wondering if the students appreciated the beauty of their surroundings and if their own moral beauty has grown apace. Or if they realize what a privilege it is to live and study in a place that was created with great care?

After the church ceremonies, I needed a ride back to the Inn at St. Mary's where I was staying. I found myself on the steps with a man a bit older than myself. He volunteered that he was a cousin of the new president and had come from Fort Wayne for the occasion which, he opined, was a grand one for their extended family. I was still carrying my academic robes on my arm as he informed me that the president, who had been a nun for twenty-five years, was married to a former priest.

A good guy, he said, who would gladly return to the practice of the priesthood if the Church would relent its rules, Besides, there was already such a scarcity of priests in his area of the Midwest that some parishes already had to be closed. None of this was said in an adversative way, but he seemed to want to elicit some response from me. I told him I thought the Pope was dancing with the Devil on this one, and he looked at me kind of funny, and said no more. I would have explained to him what I meant but it was too hot, so I didn't bother. He would not have agreed with me in any case.

*　　*　　*　　*

> I oftimes think of home, de –ol- e-ay
> While I am all alone and far away
> I sing that old refrain de-ol-e-ay
> That now recalls for me the bygone days…

The news from home is fairly uniform these days. mother seems to have stabilized again somewhat at a fairly low ebb. Now she is almost consistently refusing food, and sometime liquids too, even water. Martha says that she shakes her head vigorously when she catches sight of a cup or a glass. The only exception she makes is to take a little drink after her pills. Somehow, she knows that is necessary.

Last week it was becoming a game of cat and mouse as far as the nourishment is concerned. My niece or sister would sit with a syringe filled with water, and when mother fell asleep, and her jaw slackened, they would pop the contents of the syringe into her mouth. Some days she has taken some Ribena or fortified drink, sometimes honey and milk. There are times when she seems absolutely adamant about taking nothing.

When I returned I called my sister to find out what mother's condition was like. There is something new, she says, in that she has asked a number of people to lift her in the last day or so. Since she used to do this often when there was a lot of liquid in her lungs, my sister asked me if I thought the *"Lift me"* was as sign that the lungs

144

were filling again. I said that it might be so, if the old request was making itself vocal again after a surprising absence. Time to check with the doctor again.

I am aware that the time is getting shorter, and even though I have been through this before, I do not know what my reaction will be.

There are some things I was hoping for during these last months of mother's illness. Mostly, they all involved some commitment or other that I had made. I do not like to back out of my commitments and generally don't, with the exception of my commitments to God, which I take lightly enough, if I am under the sway of some vice or desire that has to have its day.

All in all, I am more faithful to human commitments but since some of them arise from my ministry, God gets included in them eventually. This past month it was Mary Keeney's wedding and the visit of Cardinal Silvestrini. Then it was Sister Lucille's inauguration at Rivier College. Lucille was an ACE Fellow for a year, working out of my office while she studied the governance system at Stonehill. It was in preparation for her becoming president of Rivier College the following year.

I always said that there was a possibility that I would not be able to honor these different things, if I got called away, but nobody took me seriously and I found myself getting by the commitments one by one, and heaving a sigh of relief. Only Lucille, who leaves nothing to chance, asked me if had a backup plan for her inauguration, or if there was someone else who could read the text for me. I laughed and said I didn't think there would be need for a backup.

What I didn't tell her was that the text was not finished and I could not give it to someone else to read. Martin, to whom I had showed it, said the ending was too abrupt. So I said I would include some more *"signs of the times"* in it, and then bring it to its ending. I did that, was sorry that the signs of the times were a bit negative, but they were my own perceptions, so what else could I do? I finished the piece on Friday night and e-mailed the completed version to Martin and Romelle. The journey to Nashua would come early in the morning, so I took my medication and went to bed, made a few phone calls and fell asleep.

In Donegal, at 4.30 a.m. on Saturday morning, my brother Hugh stirred in his sleep and made to get up to help Margaret change my mother. It was his habit to do this every morning around the same time.

His movement wakened his wife Sheila who was lying by his side. *"Hugh"*, she said drowsily, *"there is no need for you to go up to help Margaret this morning. Marion is down for the weekend and she is sleeping in the next room"*. Hugh had his pants on now and was sticking his feet into the shoes. *"I'll go up anyway"*, he said, *"to see what is going on"*.

It would have to be Hugh who caught the rustling sounds of tinfoil and glory in his soul that morning. He was always the clairvoyant one in the family, and he took his dreams seriously, as predictors of the future. This darkened morning, with the tide ebbing below the house, and the first cries of the curlew echoing in his ears, he was the discoverer of the past.

When he entered the room above, Margaret was sleeping quietly by my mother's side. My mother's face and hands were still warm, but the life had gone out of her. Hugh caught her wrist and felt anxiously for her pulse. He detected none, so he put his ear to her mouth and his hand on her heart. He knew she was gone, and with the blood pounding heavily in his chest, he tugged gently at the blanket that covered my sister Margaret. *"It's all over"*, he whispered gently to her as she opened her eyes. *"Oh no Hughie"*, she cried as his words sunk into her heart, *"she didn't slip away on me"*.

At Stonehill, five hours, three thousand miles, and another day away, the ringing of the telephone was like a summons from the dead. As I dragged myself into a sitting position, I looked at the clock. It was 11.49 p.m. on Friday night, and my first reaction was one of annoyance that anyone would call me that late.

It was John. He said *"Hughie just called me to say it's all over"*. The words sounded like molten lead which poured into my leaden ears and into a leaden heart. I can't much recall what I said in response, but the conversation that ensued was about the wake and the funeral. I recall saying that I would be on the plane the following night. From somewhere to somewhere - I did not know.

But Maggie's passage was becoming clear to my numbed mind. The words of the song I had sung for her in August were going to come true.

> "My barque leaves the harbor tomorrow...
> Across the wide ocean to go...
> And Kitty, my burden of sorrow...
> Is more than I wish you to know."

What next? I had to sleep because of Lucille's inauguration talk. Already, I had noted my satisfaction that I would be able to deliver it after all. But now there are other things to do.

> "There's a dreary dark cloud hangin' o'er me
> And a mighty big load on my mind...
> When I think of the prospects before me...
> and the country I'm leavin' behind."

I could see Mary Duggan heaving out the lines of the song down in Brigid's long ago. The night of a party before the Scotties went back to Glasgow. There were always parties and we always sang sad songs. There was never any party food. Just tea and bread somewhere at the end of the night.

The journey to Nashua next day with Diane, my administrative assistant, was in the rain. A sad day's rain after a long drought. I was glad for the grass and the trees and everything that was caught up in the itchy dryness. Sorry for myself that the rain could not reach my heart to alleviate the cracked dryness that spread far and wide inside me. Sorry that I could feel no emotion, just a steely will that I must hurry to do what I had to do.

After John's call a few hours before, I had fallen asleep from sheer numbness. I felt that way when I awoke. I just knew I must go.

So this was death? It came only to keep a head-hold on my emotions, letting nothing escape. Taste its embers, taste nothing. No gladness for her release, no sadness for her green going, *no nothing*.

If the universe comes from the void, then I have enough to cover for several universes, those of the past and those of the days to come. De rien, da nada, ex nihilo - at times it is more palpable than being. The meager stoicism - one could never qualify it as hope - of Beckett came to mind, *"I can't go on. You'll go on. I'll go on"*. I was driving fast on the slick roads, flirting a bit with my own mortality. But it contained my spirit somewhat. Speed always seems to help with the numbness inside.

Maybe this was to be my taste of mother's death. I had fretted about not being able to do anything for her - except pray - and I had noticed the downdrag which the daily news of her condition had on my insides.

"I think those two are kindred souls". Martin's mother Nell had made that remark to him some months ago about my mother and me.

I recall being flattered at the time because of her deep faith, what Tillich calls *"the courage to be"*. But maybe it also meant that because kindred, I had to go down with her into the deep.

Frank Walsh had delivered a piece in the chapel sometime last spring. It was about death. It ran counter to what most Christians think about the experience of death. He said things about the way death annihilates a person's total being, and that one has to pass into the darkness first. Whatever came after, the passage of darkness had to come first. *No instant resurrection in this preacher's story.* No near death experiences either. Endless like the wipers going back and forth on the wet windscreen, endless like the drops that were never wiped away. Endless....

*   *   *   *

> It was my mother who taught me how to pray,
> And to her memory my soul shall stray;
> And when I'm all alone or on my way,
> I sing that old refrain, De – o- le – ay.

When she first got sick after Christmas, it was the flu that took her badly. Then a lung infection, then a congestive heart failure situation. Early on in this process, my sister Martha called me to say that mother had taken a *"turn"* that day, but seemed to have recovered from it, and was feeling better when evening came.

I remember a saying that mother used to have that was code for warning us against ever sending her to a hospital. *"I have wings"*, she would say, *"and I am ready to fly out of here anytime"*. We took her at her word about her readiness - if not about the wings. So when Martha told me about the *"turn"* and that she was okay again, I said, *"Go in and tell her that she should not plan to fly out anywhere, because she is not on my schedule"*. mother had a good sense of humor, and she would understand what I meant, and perhaps smile at the silliness of the message.

The next day when I telephoned to see how she was, I asked my sister how mother had taken my comment. *"She did not understand* it", she said, "so I had to translate". "And what did you say?", I pressed. *"I whispered into her ear',* Martha said, *"that Bartley said not to be planning to die or anything like that, because he does not have time to come home".*

It was only a joke, and meant to take the seriousness out of the *"turn"* she had taken the previous day. But it was partially true. I had a whole springtime and summer and fall of commitments, some for helping out in parishes, some for weddings, some for matters having to do with the Capital Campaign which would be in its last months. I am not able to recall them all now, but I do remember the feeling of hope that mother would live till after this event, or that event.

In the meantime, I took no chances; my bag was packed at Easter and it stayed that way until I had to make the final trip.

*   *   *   *

From this valley they say you are going,
we will miss your bright eyes and sweet smile;
for they say you have taken the sunshine,
that brightened our pathway awhile...

Looking back on it now, I have a strange feeling that she did honour something in those last six months. I know it was not my work schedule. I will be the first to assert that no one dies for our convenience, but when the news came of her death, it seemed to me that the time ahead was easily scrubbed of the serious personal commitments that I had made. At the college, someone else can step in for you and simply say you had to go home because of your mother's death. Sr. Lucille's inaugural homily was the last thing I had laid on myself, and I was able to do it and still fly the Atlantic that night.

Now there are commitments laid on me, or ones that I take on myself, but it doesn't seem to matter anymore, because the urgency of being *'disponible'*, as the French say, is no longer there, and there is an emptiness that stretches way into the future because she is not there.

Perhaps that is the way we are meant to envisage that the next event of any importance will be our own death. I mean only to say this: that love dictates the order of our own vision, so that what is cut off from us reveals *a huge gash in the trunk of our own being.*

Elizabeth Jane Howard in *A Different Woman*, puts it like this, *"Parents, however old they and we grow to be, serve among other things to shield us from a sense of our doom. As long as they are around, we can avoid the fact of our mortality; we can still be innocent children"*. Others say, we do not become fully adult till both parents are dead. It is almost the same as Howard without stretching the truth in it.

*　　*　　*　　*

Darling, I am growing old
Silver threads among the gold;
Shine upon my brow today
Life is fleeting fast away...

Martin McGovern and Hossein Kazemi went home with me from Boston to Dublin. At the departure gates for Carrickfinn International Airport we met my cousins Noël and Pádraig O'Dubhgáin of *Clannad* along with Daniel O'Donnell. They were headed down to Mum's funeral too. Daniel was one of mother's favourite people and he came to visit every Christmas Eve with a box of chocolates for her. He remembered how she always came to Kincasslagh Hall for his concerts when he first started out - young and unknown. His loyalty to her never waned, and she would be greatly pleased that he sang at her funeral Mass.

She would also be pleased that Máire Brennan, Enya and Deirdre were there, along with the twins, Noel and Padraig. mother followed Clannad's star from the beginning, and Enya's star when it began its own ascent. Enya would stop in to see her occasionally when she came by private plane to Carrickfinn. Máire and the others did the same. She loved their visits and she loved them - and they knew it.

The Mass was a bit long because of my habit of never hurrying the liturgy, at least not this one. My cousin Baba Brennan played the organ, and she had the help of her famous family to do the singing. There were lots of priests concelebrating, Mother's great-nephew Fr. Martin Doohan, Fr. Ivan Tonge one of Tadgh's friends from Dublin and Frs. Herrity, Green, Curran, Sweeney and Meehan from the contiguous parishes.

We had to go to the graveyard afterwards to put the coffin in the hole John had dug for it. My father was the first to go into that particular plot. I have noticed now at American funerals that the undertakers not only have the green indoor/outdoor throws around the grave, but they have them draped down the sides of the grave, in case anyone would see *newly-cut earth* or *clay*, and probably faint or have to take another valium.

In Ireland the liturgy calls for the priest to let the first shovel of clay fall upon the coffin. This is one of the most neuralgic points at all funerals, especially hard on women, who hear the thud of finality with the words *"Dust to Dust, Ashes to Ashes"*, intoned by the celebrant. At the sound of the gravel hitting the wood, there is a new round of weeping, but at least it is proportionate to the loss and to the finality of death. The people do not mind taking life and death in full stride - just as they take the Atlantic in full force when it wants to put on a show.

I was acutely aware that I - who came enfleshed from the earth of her body - was returning my own life-giver to the earth, in some kind of sacral paradox. I am not sure I heard the sound of the spadeful of clay and gravel that I let fall on her coffin. Suddenly her grandchildren took over. It was their role to fill the grave and it is part of their rite of manhood to do this quickly and well. Their new shoes and the bottoms of their best trousers would get mucked-up from having to staunch the wound of the grave. We prayed during the time they did this.

The day we laid Maggie to rest in the tilted acres above Annagry Church was a day that opened the hearts of many people to love. It could not have been otherwise. When the jar of perfume is broken, its fragrance fills the whole room. Hugh opined in his remarks that we should all expect a renewal in our lives through her passing, for as the seed dies to regenerate new growth, that growth should be evident in us who were bereaved.

Of course, when it comes to moral renewal, everyone has this hope that it will occur in the others, and even could provide a detailed explanation of the areas where growth or change was desirable. I suppose most of us thought instinctively of the grandchildren, and how nice it would be if some of them "settled down", especially the long-distance runners, and the couch potatoes.

After the funeral I went over to Paddy's house to lay my throbbing head on the pillow. I could not describe my emotions because they betrayed me on that day. Perhaps they will catch me on the rebound and make me grieve in another way. I just hope that it is not through depression.... I was telling my brother Jim, who lives in London, in a letter after I got back to America that death does not move me anymore. Perhaps it is because I have seen too much of it lately. I do know that I will miss Maggie's presence when I return home... that will be another story.

*   *   *   *

Now don't you go till I come he said
And don't you make any noise...
And he toddled off to his trundle bed
And dreamt of his little toys.

While I was lying down in Paddy's house, one of the children came over to tell me that Diane, my administrative assistant at Stonehill, had called. It was about the death of a child, a sudden death, one-and-a-half years old, that belonged to Kingsley and Claire Aikins. Claire needed to talk about some things, made urgent by the fact that Kingsley was in New Zealand on Ireland Fund business.

The news numbed me, and my first reaction was that this was too sad for me to handle barely a few hours after Mother's funeral. My second reaction was to think of Claire alone in Boston and in need. I would not put off the call, so I slid off the bed to my knees, and said, *"Please, Mother, help me to say words that will be helpful to Claire, and that will be real"*.

I knew that I had no strength of my own to extend, and any words of consolation that I might attempt would be empty because I did not have any soul left to give them substance. But I also knew that it was all right for me to speak out of this condition of poverty of spirit. God had helped me before in worse situations, and now I had mother to back me as well.

The moment made me reflect on how death could be so different in its appearances: it was welcome in my Mother's case, to some extent, because of her age and her extreme weakness. But here in the death of Finlay Aikins, *it was a thief.*

I called Claire. She was composed but it was because I got her at a moment when she was between the *'up and down'* rollercoaster that painful reality initiates in the mind. Kingsley was still in New

Zealand, but she wanted some suggestions on a service for baby Finlay, where we could have it, and what it might be like. I had some thoughts on the matter, but told her that I would be home on Wednesday afternoon and that I would come by to discuss the funeral service with herself and Kingsley.

I left Donegal the next afternoon with Hossein. Martin had already gone before us to Dublin where we would catch the plane for Boston the next day. Leaving home was always difficult, but this time I was leaving a great emptiness behind, not only in our home, but also in the hearts of Martha, Hugh and Sheila, Paddy, Kathleen and John.

However, I knew that the renewal of which Hugh spoke about at my mother's funeral would make them kinder to each other than ever before. Jim's visits from London, and Tadhg's from Dublin would be looked forward to more than ever, as would the comings and goings of the grandchildren. Life in Calhame would be hard to imagine *without the observer at our window, but it would go on....*

Tom Kennedy from the Ireland Fund met me at the Boston airport. He was also meeting a friend of Kingsley's who was on the same plane. He asked me if I would like to go with them to see Kingsley and Claire. I opted to go home to freshen up, but promised to call on them that evening. When I did, there were only two others in the home. I asked Claire and Kingsley if I could see them alone. Once alone, I asked them to renew their love for each other, and never to allow Finlay's death to become a cause for blame or guilt or recrimination. They readily did this with great tenderness, which comforted me as well as themselves.

While they were doing this, I asked them to hold the crucifix that mother had held in her hands every waking moment since I had given it to her at Easter. It was a copy of a pectoral cross, which Enrico Manfrini had made for Pope John Paul II to give to all the bishops of the Great Church on their *ad limina* visits to the Holy See. When I protested to Enrico that I could not wear it, he said, *"Padre Bartolomeo, tu sei piu di un vescovo! You are more than a bishop in my eyes"* This is how my informal elevation to Manfrini's hierarchy took place in his studio in Milan.

*   *   *   *

Afterwards in Rome, I had the Pope surreptitiously bless the object that was reserved to his own giving. This was achieved simply by being in an open-air audience where he blessed religious objects anyone held up for that purpose. When I got to Ireland, I gave it to mother on the grounds that the same Pope once said *"an ounce of mother is worth a ton of priests"*. On that basis, she was at least worth a few bishops. She knew nothing of this prattle, but the crucifix became her treasure until she died.

Returning home from Claire and Kingsley's, I walked into Hafström House to find the obituary page from that day's *New York Times* lay out on my kitchen table. Diane had put a yellow marker on the notice she meant me to read. It was for Edmond Moriarty, a prince of a man who worked for Merrill Lynch and who once had done a major testimonial for Stonehill at the Waldorf-Astoria. Disbelief again filled my soul, as I let my eye fall on the time and place of wake and funeral. It was the next morning at 10.00 a.m., and the places were New Vernon and Basking Ridge in New Jersey. I did not know where those places were, and I knew I could never get there in time, without aggravating my back. Yet, I got my Rand-McNally out and looked up both places. One I could not find, but the other was somewhat east of Newark. I wished I had someone to send.

Next morning, the dull low pain that is peculiar to the lumbar discs woke me at 5.30 a.m. I lay there for a few minutes assessing my possibilities. I had a choice of pumping myself full of medication or heading for the airport.

A few hours later I was in Basking Ridge at the funeral home. Ginny Moriarty was surprised to see me because when they had called about Ed's death, they were told I was in Ireland at my mother's funeral. I met all the children and their spouses. The Moriartys have to be one of best-looking families in the whole United States, and their dad had left them too soon.

The time was near for departure to the church and one of Ed's friends, a priest who had gone to school with him, asked me if I wanted to do one of the readings from the New Testament. It was from Luke:

> *"I thank you, Father, for what you have hidden from the wise and clever, you have revealed to mere children... Come to me, all you who are heavy burdened and I will give you rest. Take up your yoke and learn from me for I am weak and humble of heart. And you'll find rest for your souls, for my yoke is easy and my burden is light".*

It was the same text I had chosen to read for my mother's Mass of Resurrection, and I smiled inwardly with great joy as I read it. Later on, I asked Fr. Murray if I could say a few words of eulogy about Mr. Moriarty. He hesitated, because he said there were already several family members lined up to speak, and the church would be filled with Wall Street folks anxious to get back to the turmoil of the markets, but then he said yes.

I was brief. I said why I felt compelled to come and say what I had to say namely that the goodness and integrity of this great man was out of the ordinary, as were his modesty and generosity. Ginny and the family looked very proud of him, and they had a right to be. There will not be too many others like him at Merrill Lynch - or anywhere else for that matter. I returned home after Mass.

*   *   *   *

The Saturday after my return, there was a service in St. Cecilia's in the Back Bay for Finlay Francis Aikins. He was one and a half when he died in his cot, his father in New Zealand and his mother in the next room. Kingsley and Claire were devastated by the loss, but they had many good friends who came to St. Cecilia's for the funeral service.

I said what I could, and prayed that they might find some comfort in it. I repeated the text I had used at Mother's funeral Mass. Now I know from experience that the words, *"Come to me all you who labor and are heavy-burdened and I will give you rest..."* are accepted directly by many people in emotional stress or bereavement and the preacher does not need to go on about it. *They are the words of Jesus, his own personal invitation* - and they have a direct effect of their own on those who believe in Him. For Claire and Kingsley, I know the presence of their friends and the balloons Clare tied to his casket, as well as the beauty of the old basilica, did something to kill the heartache all of us were feeling.

Afterwards, I stood with Fr. Peter Walsh on the steps outside St. Cecilia's as Claire and Kingley's friends were departing. A tall black woman came passing by on the street above the Church. She was stunningly dressed with a headpiece of gold lamé, kerchief-style on her braided hair. She did not even turn towards us as she passed by, and exclaimed to no one in particular – because there was only us - *"I once saw a woman spit in the chalice in Terre Haute, Indiana"*. To say anything back to the lady would have been something like *lèse majesté*. I muttered something under my breath, but Peter, sensing my need to go on the stage with her, said *"Say nothing, Bartley, for God's sake or she will come after us"*. The queen passed us by, regnant, in her great beauty. I said nothing.

* * * *

What the Dying Orchid said...

She sits in her high backed chair
gazing out at the sunset,
in her lap a book,
in her resting hand
a magnifier. Her face and hair glow
suffused with the salmon light
of the fading sun. A smile
stirs on her face
like a slight breeze touching a petal.
She is watching light
wash through the rows of cloud
with its smooth fervor. Some,
caught in her eyes, mingles,
with a private fire, becomes one flame,
one phoenix candle, this one not setting,
not consumed.

                                 - Paul O. Williams

Pat Mortati does many household chores inside and out for Don and Beverly Flynn down in Boca Raton, Florida. What is not a chore for Pat is looking after the orchid plants, which have become his pride and joy and passion. Many of the plants start off as gifts to the Flynns, but Pat keeps them long after they have served their use, and nourishes them into another life. His alchemy looks like nothing more than the proverbial green thumb and the old tender loving care.

One day I was reading in the courtyard where his plants are spread around in different locations. Suddenly, he shouted out - to me, I suppose, because I was the only one there - *"Look, look"!* he said, *"the orchid is dying"!* I hurried over to see what had so excited him. *"See"*, he said, *"the orchid plant is killing itself to send out more flowers"*. Sure enough, the orchid was dying - but it had sent forth a stem of new blossoms.

If the plant could talk, I would have asked it why it was killing itself, or why - in the act of dying - it was sending our last stem of glorious flowers. Then it occurred to me that this was a stupid thought, because my question would have to be in words - the fruit of reason - while the orchid's answer would have to have be in its mute beauty - a beauty which takes the breath of reason away.

I will never forget the orchid plant. I have thought of it so many times - and I have thought of it as an icon for the *"extra"* time that Maggie remained alive from Easter till October. She had said quite clearly, as I remarked in my e-mail message for March 22, that she said she wanted to get better and so she would have to start praying. It would be silly on my part to assign a motive to her desire. The will to live is too strong to be assigned motives. One could have a hundred motives and still not have the will. *But it was a season for putting out beauty when there was virtually nothing of her left.* None of us who saw it could ever forget.

*   *   *   *

In a pastoral letter to his people for the millennium, the Cardinal Archbishop of Milan, Carlo Maria Martini, says that he sought a long time for an icon that would unify his thoughts. What kept coming back to him again and again, was a scene from *The Idiot* by Dostoyevsky. In the scene the atheist Ippolit asks Prince Myskin, *"Is it true, O Prince, that you have said that one day the world will be saved by Beauty? Gentlemen - he cried out loudly to everyone -the Prince affirms*

that one day the world shall be saved by beauty…
What kind of beauty will save the world?"

It is a mocking question, and similar to the one that Pilate asked Jesus, *"What is truth"?* Jesus did not answer the cynical question, and neither does Myskin. It would seem that his silence - which accompanies an infinite compassion of love for the youth of eighteen who is dying of consumption - wishes to say *that the beauty which saves the world is the love that is willing to share sorrow.*

This could also be a small icon of the beauty of Maggie's love which became compassion when faced with another's suffering. It is a tiny little flower of the of the immense Beauty of which Augustine cries when his love has been purified, *"Late have I found Thee, O Thou Beauty, ever ancient and ever new".*

On the way to God's glory our icon is not the beauty that seduces, but the moral beauty that saves. This is why the Love of Christ who was born *"in the beauty of the lilies … with a glory in his bosom that was meant for you and me…"* will always remain the supreme icon of the moral beauty which shares our sorrow and our burdens until the death. The dead wood of his Cross becomes a tree of life - a tree of enormous life-giving beauty for all who need even the smallest ray of a vision for their journey. We have the capacity to be that beauty, too, whenever we lighten each other's burden, whenever our love can become compassion - not pity - in the face of another's suffering. The reward of blessedness here is simply a cup of cold water to slake another's thirst.

*   *   *   *

Last year, J. J. Lyons had given me a book by Máire B. de Paor. It is called *Patrick, the Pilgrim Apostle of Ireland.* "Here", he said, *"take it, because I can't make heads nor tails of it"*. I did not pay immediate heed to the book, but later browsed through a few pages of the text, and right away I knew I had a mighty work of scholarship on my hands. I read the *Confessio* in the Latin and English, and followed the meticulous notes, which the author had provided.

I came to the passage, which de Paor calls the crux of one of the most mysterious passages in the whole of hagiography – the writings of the saints – and it is Patrick's vision of the Holy Spirit praying within him. He is at prayer and suddenly he becomes conscious of the Spirit praying within him: The passage reads:

> And again, I saw him PRAYING within myself
> And I was, as it were inside my own body,
> And I heard [him] over me, this is [to say], over the interior person
> And THERE HE WAS earnestly with groans,
> And admidst these things 'I was astonished and I kept wondering and thinking'....

I had the got fortune to meet Sister Maire de Paor in Falmouth, on Cape Cod, the following summer and I could not believe my good fortune. I was to give a talk on St. Patrick at the Irish Cultural Festival at Stonehill the following day, and it was mostly to discuss the findings of her new study. There were some elements in the sequence of events of which I was unsure, so I asked her to lead me briefly through the main points of Patrick's story.

When we had finished, I told her about this memoir, and brought up the experience of my mother's prayer in the spirit. She asked me if I had read her footnote from St. John on the Cross on Patrick's mystical experience. I told her I had, but that it seemed to have no relevance to my experience.

When I returned home that evening, I read the reference again, to see if it were helpful. It was not. The quotation was about *"vision"* and *God's abstracting the spirit and providing the bodily functions himself*

- all of this, of course, was in the context of the intervention of God in the life of a dying person.

There was no vision in my mother's experience, as far as I could tell, but there was an awesome experience of prayer. As far as *"God's abstracting the spirit and providing the bodily functions himself"*, I would have no way of validating this statement. mother remained an invalid, but at a somewhat higher level of stability, which I cannot compare with any other medical state. Frankly, at times we wondered what was keeping her ravaged body together.

At the suggestion of my cousin, Olivia Gallagher Connolly, whom I saw in Donegal this summer, I sent the first three chapters to Fr. Joe Glynn, OCD, at the Carmelite Abbey in Loughrea, Co. Galway. He responded by saying he had enjoyed reading the account I had written about the Easter experience. He added that it was a great grace to pass from this world by so much love, care and prayer from community and family. Then he surprised me with these words, at the bottom of the first page of his letter:

"When we come to write about the experience of your mother's prayer, we enter secret and mysterious ground. We should take off our shoes. The words of St. John of the Cross may cast some light on the subject. I just hope they help".

Then he quoted the passage from St. John of the Cross:

'There is a high form of prayer, when, the Will stops making acts of love on its own. God makes acts of love in it. He inebriates it secretly with infused love. These acts are much more delightful and meritorious than the acts the soul makes on its own, just as God who moves it and infuses this love is much better'. (Living Flame 3:50)

Fr. Joe moved on to apply the more familiar words of the Scriptures, from the Letter of Paul to the Galatians 2:20.

"I died to the law, that I might live for God.

"I (ego) have been crucified with Christ,.

"yet I live : no longer I, but Christ lives in me".

One can move on from this powerful passage to assert its easily drawn corollaries:

"yet I love: no longer I, but Christ loves in me...."

"yet I pray: now not I, but Christ prays in me......"

I was grateful for being led to the passages in Scripture and also for the passage from John of the Cross which, at least, seemed apposite to the experience which my mother had. When the paradigm for living in Christ, loving in Christ, praying in Christ – when the paradigm is established, it is not a wonder that this form of prayer can, and does, happen. The wonder really is - that it doesn't happen more often.

*   *   *   *

Epilogue

Shall we gather by the river
The beautiful, beautiful river -
Gather with the saints at the river
That flows by the throne of God

Dear Maggie:

I have been carrying this memoir around in my computer for the better part of two years now. I have gone over it endless times to make sure it said what I intended it to say - about you and about us. I never even thought about writing anything until I heard you praying to God for your life with such intensity. Then I knew I had to put some of our *Easter experience* down on paper, so that people would take courage from it.

You know the last thing I want to do is to make you into some kind of an icon. That would distort you, because icons are formal, stylized, angular - and they lack expression. You were none of the above, you were too interested in life, in people and politics, in crosswords, St. Anthony's pools and snooker. You were also too much fun and good company, and if I do not get your portrait done with all your human qualities, then I will have failed. *Bhí tú íontach nadúrtha!* as Hugh said on your funeral day. *You were very well natured!*

At the same time, I know that you would not mind my drawing attention to the things God had done in your life, and that in your faithfulness to Jesus, your Brother and Saviour, you were able - somehow - to infect others with the *joy and wonder* that marked your own life That is why I would like this book to be read by ordinary people because it is to them that you speak.

I have put some of my own reflections into the memoir, only because I would like some of my colleagues in the academy to look seriously at the choices of life and death which we lay before our students. If frogs were being born deformed or dying, there would be a big furore about pesticides and the like. When young people are growing up morally deformed - without a clue about life, its meaning or its possible meaning - no one seems to know how to deal with it.

The young know no ethical codes, only rules to prevent them from getting in trouble; they know no faith and have no paradigms or stories that would help them identify and cope with adversity. They have only a shallow range of positive emotions, and they do not have the words to describe their condition - but they do know the negative emotions much better: rage and hatred, resentment and fear – and the way to express those feelings is frequently through violence.

The time for reading, reflection and research is for me still wide open and inviting, but I know if I do not couple it with the search for simplicity and moral freedom that marked your life, I will be left standing at the starting post of an unfinished and mediocre life. And I am bothered by the plight of the young, especially those who are chained by their compulsions and addictions - not to mention those who do not see anything lovable about life, and do not know how to name their sadness.

Perhaps your story - even though you are so far removed from them - will help them in some way, and help others to reach out to them.

There are so many books on spirituality in the market these days, and it is obvious that many people are feeling hunger in their hearts. Many of them have nice thoughts and meditations, but they do not offer a simple program for living. The way to the *simplicity and freedom* should be coupled with an equally simple program of prayer, meditation and action. Fuzzy feelings are not enough, and I believe many books on the market are of the *"feel-good"* spirituality type. They are the equivalent of spiritual valium.

It is no secret that trying to achieve greater union with God is difficult - and people are afraid of it because they know it means a measure of suffering. But growth into union with God is really *the only option* before us. The alternative is to observe with horror as life flows through our hands - and we come to view time as our enemy. Heidegger was right in his observation that time has become the enemy for modern man.

St. John of the Cross said, *"In the evening of our lives, we shall be judged on love"*. He was only echoing his Master who said that what we do to the least of his brothers and sisters, we do unto Him. This is the anonymous Christ who is to be found in all our lives; his message is not tied to any creed or colour or social standing.

During the last months of your betterment, I often wondered what made you decide to want to get better. Was it for the sake of some of us who were not yet prepared to see you go? Or were you - without knowing it - forging among us something that would happen after you were gone? Was it a surprise to yourself that your will to live was stronger than you ever thought? The thought even crossed my mind that you were too polite to die - after Claire came all that way from California to see you!

I think if I had an *epiphany* about our reunion, I would prefer it to be on the river, and I would like to see you captain *The Derry*

Boat out of port to the Great Ocean of Life when we finally get under way. We will hardly be at the front of the parade, but I don't think we will be at the end of it either.

As Flannery says, all those folks who had less than us will have to come before us. That is also the way the Gospel says it has to be. That means Hanningan the tramp and all the tinkers who stopped in our shop to ask for help.

Frank and Fan McCool will be ahead of us too - and all the lonely people who came to you on Sunday afternoons to warm themselves at the fire of your love. There will be slaves from many lands, wearing their manacles of gold, and they will be singing *"How blest we are …"* There will come a huge crowd which we will be unable to count. These are *the wretched of the earth* - those who thought God had forgotten them in their time – the victims of the Holocaust, the Gulags and the Great Hunger.

The dwarfs, misfits and marplots, the compulsives and the long-distance runners will certainly be ahead of us, and so would all the folk who were stunted in their psychosexual growth; all the children from broken marriages, young women whose lives were thwarted in love; all the addicts - the alkies, the narcs, the gamblers, anorexics, pedophiles, kleptos – the stutterers and the hare-lipped, as well as those who had shaking diseases all during their lives.

The Derry Boat will probably be glorified too - like our cowbyre in the painting - despite the disgrace it was to the human race when Burns & Laird ran it as an emigrant boat for us and for the all the cattle it carried down below. It showed the high opinion they had of us on our way to Glasgow.

It will be our boat now - and even the meanest among us will sparkle. It will be a testimony to how we survived *this bent world*, and we will finally know that God did not make it that way, and that the Spirit always renews the face of the earth despite our attempts to mar it. You always knew that – didn't you?

"There lives the dearest freshness deep down things...
Because the Holy Ghost over the bent
World broods with warm heart and with ah! bright wings."

It will be interesting to see how many generations will be aboard. I hope your Olphert ancestor is aboard - and her fisherman husband - so that we can get a glimpse of how close we missed the line of royalty in the neighbouring islands.

I believe that after death there will be such a thing as *a journey into God*. This, simply because of the depth and immensity of God. Obviously, I cannot say it will be a journey measured by time, because time will be no more. We will go from glory into glory, until our vision which begins like that of the owl blinded by light, becomes like that of the eagle whose eyes can look directly at the sun.

This journey seems necessary because, at death, most of us are not prepared to see God. The journey will be purifying, but the purification will be mitigated by our consciousness of blessedness. Aquinas tried to express this journey as *"aeveternity"*. This is not commonly accepted now, but something like it has to be conceived. Put simply, Stalin and mother Teresa are not ushered *into the beatific vision* immediately at the moment of death.

For this journey into God, we will probably *be gathered to those* with whom we share some spiritual kinship and - since we do not know our influence for good on others - it will be interesting to see *who else is joined to our group*. We would expect them to be on the Derry Boat too.

Without a doubt, there will also be people quite surprised to see us too, because they may have thought, in this life, that we were definitely headed south - to Dixie.

I thought you would like to see this quote which I kept for the end of the book. It is from Louis Evely's book *"On Brotherhood"*:

"It is impossible to pass on to others your good qualities; they belong entirely to you, and that causes humiliation to others. ONLY GOD IS COMMUNICABLE. And we must give souls anything less than Him. If you are a living witness to others of the great things God has been able to do in our nothingness; if while longing to go away, you nevertheless remain; and if, while feeling yourself incapable and at the of your resources, you still hold on - then you will be able to give others something far better than yourself: you can give them Him whom you have found."

Maggie, this is how I think you did it! And we are glad for you, and grateful for your life with us.

Love!

Bartley

*   *   *   *

Reflections

In the course of writing this memoir which, like memory itself, is not terribly well organised, I wrote two chapters that are in the realm of reflection or meditation. I offer them both at the end of this book.

The first simply outlines the importance of the child's mother for the longest journey a child will ever make - into an awareness of itself as free and secure and as unique.

The second is my own existential cocktail on how I see the achievement of simplicity and moral freedom. They allow a person to live life fully, but they do not come without cost. I see both arising from the human condition much as I saw them in my mother's life - a combination of nature and grace.

I hope this little book finds its way into the hands of those who need it.

The Longest Journey

"Summertime was nearly over, blue Italian skies above;
I said, 'Lady I'm a rover …
Can you spare me just one word of love…
She whispered softly 'twas best not to linger,
And as I kissed her hand, I could see…
She wore a plain golden ring on her finger,
'Twas goodbye to the Isle of Capri…"

A child's first impressions of the world are the surest, but they are the least recoverable to memory. There is only one sense operative at birth. It is the tactile sense, and there is little else: no seeing, little hearing, no smelling, and blind tasting. The psychology of childhood is filled with famous names like Freud, Montessori, Piaget and Bettelheim.

Those who delve into the thicket of childhood are far from agreement on fundamental influences, and they generally bring us to a place where we can no longer follow because of their psychological jargon. Still, we are all born of woman, nourished and reared – *somehow* - and we can trace in our own fashion how it was with us.

One of my earliest impressions of mother is quite simple: it was having her all to myself. Only two people were in the ellipse of love: one was Me and the other was Her. The grammar of the description above is bad. It should be: one was I and the other was She. But if we objectify the persons, we can understand it better.

Another of my early impressions is that there came a time, which I remember quite vividly, when I became aware of someone Else who was breaking into the secure ellipse of our love. I used to slap her face to get her to give me all her attention. What I wanted her to say to me is totally forgotten and now equally unimportant.

But I remember clearly the other. She did not mind my importuning tantrums because she was praying, and would not let me restrain her.

I do not remember this experience as expulsion from the ellipse, but it was made clear to me that I had to share it with someone else. It was my first sibling rivalry. There would be others to follow. But it was possible to play games with the real siblings, to find ways of outfoxing them, with wiles too numerous to mention from the bag of tricks to which every child has access.

If childhood is open to psychology, then it is also open to philosophy. Theology can also have something to say about the meaning of the shadowy beginnings of human consciousness. The eminent Swiss theologian, Hans Urs von Balthasar, has a wonderful passage in one of his books on the significance of a child's first impressions of the world, and of the very special role the mother plays in this.

The little child, he says, wakens to self-consciousness through being addressed by the love of its mother.

Her smile and her whole gift of self, of love to love, is what the child interprets as the highest good and in itself absolutely sufficient. Relying on Martin Buber's famous "I - Thou" relationship, Balthasar goes on to explain that it is the "Thou" of the mother which brings forth the "I" of the child, and that in this moment everything is lit up with "a lightning flash of the origin with a ray so brilliant and whole that it also includes a disclosure of God".

This is heady language, and perhaps the best way to explain it is through the story of the Garden of Eden in the Bible. Adam and Eve understand that they inhabit a place that is the highest good, and in itself absolutely sufficient for their needs. They are also aware of the presence of God since the moment of their awakening to human consciousness. God is even said to walk in the garden *"in the cool of the evening"*, when the innocent and naked rapture of the young lovers, leaves room in the ellipse of their love to include their Creator. This explanation of the child's paradise with its mother is only alluded to in Balthasar's work, but I have expanded it to show that it is only through myth that we can understand our beginning and our end.

For the rest, we believe that we can interpret and understand what is *"really real"* in our adult lives, even though some philosophers have argued that we only see shadows of reality (*Plato's cave*), and poets have sung that *"we are the stuff that dreams are made of, and our lives are rounded by a little sleep"* (Shakespeare).

What I wish to underline in this rather heavy portion of a memoir is *the importance of the mother in the life of the child*. It does not choose whether to respond to love or not. It is enticed by the mother's smile *"just as the sun entices forth green growth"* because it is in venturing toward her *"Thou"* that the child becomes aware of itself as an *"I"*.

The journey toward selfhood has begun, love responds to love, and it will eventually go beyond the *"Thou"* of the mother *to the world*. In crossing this space, the child will eventually experience *"its freedom, its knowledge, its being as spirit"*.

This may be the longest and most important journey of our lives. What remains crucial in this process is the love of the mother. It will determine whether the child can succeed in identifying what is later affirmed in Christianity. It is really a stupendous assertion that, to my knowledge, is made only in Catholicism, namely: that *Being and Love are coextensive*.

This latter truth is one of which the mystics speak of, especially Lady Julian of Norwich and her vision of the hazelnut, and they speak of it as having been experienced by them. We, who do not have the privilege, are conscious of too many alienations in our own being and that of others. The problem of evil makes it almost impossible for us to experience Being and Love as one and the same.

It should be mentioned that others claim to be mystics too, but in a reverse direction. One of the best expressions of this is found in the character of *the lieutenant* (sic) in Graham Greene's *"The Power and the Glory"*. He was part of the Mexican regime that from 1926 to 1928, unleashed the worst religious persecution since the reign of Elizabeth I of England. It was the Cristero rebellion whose motto *"Viva Cristo Rey"* that led to the height of anticlericalism, while invoking Christ the King.

It infuriated the lieutenant that were still people in the state who believed in a loving and merciful God. He knew that there were mystics who were said to experience God directly. *"He (the lieutenant) was a mystic, too, and what he experienced was vacancy - a complete certainty in the existence of a dying, cooling world, of human beings who had evolved from animals for no purpose at all. He knew"*.

This raises the interesting difference between the *mystics of being* and the *mystics of nothingness*. The mystics of being have to pass through long and painful periods of experiencing nothing on their way to fuller and fuller experience of Being. On the other hand, the mystics of nihilism rarely mention the *tremendum ac fascinans* (awesomeness and fascination) of Being, or of the Holy, as Rudolf Otto described it, or even what Nietzsche himself acknowledged in his earlier years that, *"Nature's first need is for the Holy thing"*.

Perhaps both can come together in a concept found in the experience St. John of the Cross who describes God as *Todo y Nada (All and Nothing)*.

Or perhaps a new way can be found in the apophatic tradition of Eastern Christianity where God is neither posited or negated, but is simply prayed to wordlessly.

Sir John Polkinghorne who is an Anglican divine and also a particle physicist, mentioned the this apophatic (it means *wordless*) tradition of the Eastern Orthodox Churches at the Erasmus Conference recently at the University of Notre Dame. No one asked him to expand further on the idea. I feel that most participants thought it was some new element of particle physics that had been discovered. Annie Dillard gives a notion of what apophatic (wordless) prayer might mean in this passage:

> You do not have to sit outside in the dark
> If, however, you want to look at the stars,
> You will find that darkness is necessary.
> But the stars neither require nor demand it....
>
> 'The silence is all there is.
> It is the alpha and the omega.
> It is God's brooding over the face of the waters;
> it is the blended note to the ten thousand things,
> the whine of wings.
> You take a step in the right direction
> to pray to this silence,
> and even to address the prayer to "World",
> Distinctions blur.
> Quit our tents.
> Pray without ceasing.'

For the rest, the disclosure of God mentioned by Von Balthazar, as having been experienced by all of us, in the moment of consciousness may be as gratuitously asserted as denied. However, the vast mass of us, including intellectuals, do not, or care not to, reflect on the mystery of our own, individual, existence. Just as we know that the world is not necessary, we know that neither are we. *The word a-seitas, (of-it-selfness) which desribes the nature of God's being in the philosophy of John Duns Scotus, has been enough to set some great minds free from the downdrag of unbelief.*

Reflection on the unnecessity of our own being, along with the fact that WE ARE, is bound to lead us into the heart of the mystery of our own existence. Our own existence is obviously only a tiny piece of the action, but it is packed with mystery. It summons up words like destiny, fate, determinism, free will, time, potency and act, creation, evolution, intentionally, good and evil, nature and grace.

Determinism – if we believe that things have to be the way they are – takes almost all of the mystery away. If we believe in free will, even if the freedom is limited, makes for a life that is jam-packed with wonder, because the questions become deeper, more inviting.

Again, when we read the little book of Tolstoy, *The Death of Ivan Illych*, we can see how mysterious the self is, especially when it bumps up against its limits. It is what Brendan Behan would call *"the auld triangle going jingle-jangle"* or what a more sober psychiatrist-turned-philosopher, Karl Jaspers, calls *die Grenze-Situation*, or the limit-situation. The most serious limit to our being is Death.

It is worth quoting a passage from Tolstoy's story, *The Death of Ivan Illych*, to indicate emotions are shocked out of their accustomed circuits by his impending death:

"Ivan Ilych saw that he was dying, and he was in continual despair. In the depths of his heart he knew he was dying, but not only was he not accustomed to the thought, he simply did not and could not grasp it".

Ivan had learnt in his logic book the syllogism:

> 'Caius is a man,
> Men are mortal,
> And therefore Caius is mortal'

What Ivan did not realize was that the assent that he gave to this proposition which is logically true, was not *real assent*, but rather *notional assent*. The distinction is John Henry Newman's but it is helpful to us to know that we often assent to things believing that we are giving real assent, while in many cases it is *notional assent* we give, a step far removed from the real thing.

The difference between logical truth and *real truth* breaks Ivan's world into smithereens. It was okay that this Cause in the book was mortal, but he (Ivan) was not an abstract man, *"but a creature quite, quite separate from all others. He had been little Vanya, with a mamma and a papa, with Mitya and Volodya, with the toys, a coachman and a nurse, afterwards with Katenka, and with all the joys, griefs and delights of childhood, boyhood and youth. What did Caius know of the smell of that striped leather ball Vanya had been so fond of? Had Caius kissed his mother's hands like that and did the silk of her dress rustle so for Caius? Had he rioted like that at school when the pastry was bad? Had Caius been in loved like that? Could Caius preside at a session as he did?*

Caius was really mortal, and it was right for him for die; but for me little Vanya, Ivan Ilych, with all my thoughts and emotions, it's altogether a different matter. It cannot be that I ought to die. That would be too terrible."

Ivan Ilych was running into the mystery of himself. Death would be a mystery too, but it was the reality of death that sent his memory into orbit, trying to make sense of the *"I"* who had been little Vanya with a mamma and a papa and a coachman and a nurse, and who suddenly remembered striped leather balls, and the way his mother's silk dress rustled for him and who rioted at school when the pastry was bad... Now, for Ivan it was all a mystery, something that could not be understood.

ut mystery is not exactly something that blocks our understanding. A better understanding of mystery is that which allows us to penetrate deeper and deeper, even though we know that we can never exhaust its meaning or achieve full understanding of it. Just as we can never exhaust the mystery of nature or of the cosmos we inhabit, so too, we never can exhaust our own being, or the being of another. *That is why we are called persons.*

Balthasar also indicates that the *initial pure bliss* of our bond with our mothers may cause us to experience all else as deficient, failing to please us, *as loss and a falling away from happiness.* This can explain the reason why some persons cannot overcome their unhappiness, and why eventually they nourish their unhappiness as an argument, or anger, against the world, eventually against God. Kierkegaard calls this a form of despair and further points out that some people are loath to be deprived of their unhappiness because it deprives them of their argument against existence.

'Tis the gift to be simple
tis the gift to be free
tis the gift to come round
to where we ought to be...

After the Easter event, when Love entered a little house in Donegal and directed such a beautiful symphony for several months, our hearts could not be moved more, and our minds would never be the same again. For me it came down to the two words of the Shaker song: *simple and free.* They meant for me, at least, that there was a new need in my life, and that was to try to love candidly and simply - in a way that would be transparent in my being and actions. *Agere sequitur esse (Action follows Being.)* I had been too busy before - *doing things* - to think of this in a forceful way.

There was a need also to examine the other side of the question: *the need to be loved,* to find a source of love and the willingness to accept it. Most psychologists and spiritual directors will attest to the fact that being able to receive love is, in some ways, more difficult than to give love. The wisdom of our age tells us that we have to love ourselves before we can either give or receive.

Is there a source of love beyond human loves? Is there a source that is even beyond the fully human and that passes into the divine? And what does fully human mean? The answers to these questions are crucial to my living. And for those who ask them more urgently. For the young who feel them and don't even know how to ask them. Despite my own many stupidities in life, the stops and starts, the having to relearn lessons I had learnt before, these questions have pursued me and driven my life - *like a fugue* - from an early age. It was questions like these that drew me to existentialist thinking in philosophy, literature and theology. I tried to get my students to ask - and to reflect on - these same questions.

Now these questions are the same ones that so many lives, especially young lives, starved for meaning and love, are asking in mute agony and anguish. Most adults cannot recognize this need, even in their own flesh and blood. They try to pass on their own fetishes of comfort and materialism, their paradigms of success - and cannot understand why they are not enough.

There is a response, made to Satan in the wilderness - that man does not live on bread alone - but we have a hard time taking this message to heart, when there bread aplenty; *but the hunger of the heart is not stilled, and its soulful anguish cannot be named.*

If there is not an inexhaustible source, available to us in some way, love will just be a word to express *the emotional investment we have in each other.* There is a splendid example of this in the film, *"The Lion in Winter",* the tale of King Henry II of England, his wife Eleanor of Acquitaine and their three surly sons. There is no love between any of them - and all they know is how to call in the chips when their emotional investments in each other have run out.

If love turns out to be just this, then *altruism will not be possible,* and Freud will be right in his glum assessment of life: the reason we love is that we see something of ourselves in the other. *Life and love in this reading are basically narcissistic.*

In any case, I believe that all can agree on one thing: that the self reaches the limits of loving after a fairly short time. *To pray is the fastest way to realize the hardness of one's own heart,* and its inadequacy to do all the things that one feels called to do: by grace or by moral imperative, by human respect, by vow, duty, or by shame. Aquinas teaches that shame is a half-virtue, but we have become used even to the lack of half-virtues in our society. Their absence suggests that virtue in our society has feet like a daddy-long-legs.

Living, loving, behaving morally or ethically - all these things have to be done by agnostics and atheists as well as by those who live by different humanisms. They have to be done - *per forza* - by those who try to live by faith. All people reach the tether's end at some time of their human experience.

A tether makes a grazing cow go around in circles. But there are times when we need some more rope, perhaps when we come to the *Thin Place*, or *a patch of quaking-grass*, in the course of our own tethering. *"I can't go on. You'll go on. I'll go on"* is the Samuel Beckett way of stating the limits of the human tether, and the stoicism of human response.

> Beside the ocean's din she combed her hair,
> Singing the nocturne of the passing ships,
> Before her earthly lover found her there,
> And kissed away the music from her lips.

To love and to allow oneself to be loved: two things that are not easily done. Because they both run into the mystery of death, one's own death of course, and that of the significant others in our lives. It has been said that we cannot live *a free life* until we have come to terms with our own mortality. We can also say that we cannot live a *loving life* until we have, in some way, conquered the fear of death.

We know intuitively that nothingness is part of our reality as creatures. We do not want to fall back into nothingness, but the possibility of this is real enough to make anxiety a fellow traveler all our lives.

This is not new. Many thinkers, beginning with St. Augustine, Blaise Pascal, Sören Kierkegaard, continuing down to Martin Heidegger, have illustrated clearly that death sends us all a message with which we have to struggle, by accepting it, by denying it, by attempting to drown the message, or by forgetting it in busyness. But there is no killing this messenger.

And this is only one horn of the dilemma that is the human condition.

The other horn is that, as creatures, we have a desire for greater being. The *desire for knowledge* admits to an *infinite horizon*. In the modern era, the *will to pleasure, to power, and to meaning* are probably the best documented of our drives and they are well nigh insatiable. The list of our needs are like the nine-headed Hydra, which sprouted *two more* whenever Hercules cut one off. In any case needs multiply - and grow more refined, or monstrous and grotesque - as the case may be.

A massive body of myth and ritual show that we desire to commune with whatever powers we conceive as transcendent, that is to say beyond the known universe. Others conceive the ultimate power as being immanent, that is to say, within the universe. The biblical story which is the mother lode of mythical meaning for Judaism and Christianity indicates that we desire to be like gods, knowing good and evil. That was the first temptation of freedom, and it still runs through bent human history like a broken record.

Things have not changed a whole lot. Our present age has made it clear that we want to go beyond good and evil, so that we, like gods, determine what good and evil are. The line between good and evil has certainly become porous, because relativized, and the very notion of meaning is under attack in much of the academic world. *The dons never seem to learn that what is deconstructed in the mind will soon be acted out by the young who can sense nihilism more quickly than the rest of us.*

The problem that drove Friedrich Nietzsche mad is a not theoretical one. It is both practical and existential, and that means, among other things, that it forces us to make choices.

My mother knew nothing of Nietzsche and Heidegger, and it is not my intention to say that she thought in their categories or saw her life in this fashion. But these thinkers did not create the dilemma.

It is inherent in the human condition, my condition and yours. The existentialist writers or thinkers only articulate it more clearly for the people of our time.

Only the young are excluded, because more than at any other time in the history of our race, the culture in which they live prevents them from asking questions about the unexamined life. Sophisticated in other ways, their spiritual illiteracy is a yawning gap that grows apace and rankly. And they have no words to name their pain. I found my conviction of several years – a conviction born of experience and observation – better described recently by *Lawrence Raab* in a poem on *Hamlet's Problems* in the *New Republic.* It interprets Hamlet as a person who makes a joke about everything, especially death…

> "… pretends he's crazy, pretends he's sane,
> in it alone to the end. As if everything
> had turned into a joke only he understands.
> Even death. Especially death…"

Raab then universalizes the Hamlet mentality to include all those who are in it alone to the end, ending with a reflection on what this might mean in the despair of today's youth culture.

"How impoverished action looks by itself-
Some hopeless kid locked in his room
With his father's revolver. That's all
There is to it, he thinks, so fuck it.
At a loss to say what it might be.
Or any of the words that could make it matter."

The good side of existentialist thinking, as opposed to the dry rationalisms of the past, is that it puts the searchlight on the will and the emotions. It can illustrate the spiritual foundations of life and its fundamental moments. It also throws light on great moral issues of anguish and hope, despair and trust, being and nothingness. It illustrates how people react to these realities in the different stages of their lives.

Mother encountered those moments of decision like everyone else. She may have worked out her choices in a way that is perhaps easier to grasp for those will read this memoir. This may be helpful to her own children and those who loved her.

On the other hand, it may be helpful only to me. Perhaps that is why I feel impelled to write it down.

Surveying the landscapes of our lives, we can remember with clarity how, at times, we were brought into *the thin place, where the quaking-grass grows,* and how we were made free again. And how that pattern happened not once or twice, but was repeated many times over.

In earlier times, people in Donegal believed that while they were on a journey, especially through the lonely mountains, they might come across a spot where *the féar gortach* (or hungry grass) grew. Some carried a piece of bread in their pockets so that they might not be overcome by the weakness that ensued. The *féar gortach* was attributed to the little people, as *the sídhe* or the *faery-folk* were known.

Whatever about the reality of these places, it is surely well known to all that, on the journey of our lives, we do come into the thin places, where the quaking grass grows, and suddenly we discover that we have little or nothing to nourish us through the difficult patch of grass. This often happens when we are going through a period of growth, but it may appear to us as a crisis, and we may be aware only of the spiritual anguish.

Many people have sought down the years to illustrate the stages of growth we pass through from birth to death. This is done by poets and playwrights, by physicians and pediatricians, by philosophers and psychologists, and also by spiritual writers. The latter have been largely forgotten in our time, which is *so smitten by immediacy and the instantaneous.* But a long list of witnesses are still present to persuade us that there are stages of growth in the life that is given to us. To affirm that we grow in all other ways and to deny that we need to grow spiritually is a hard argument to sustain. We neglect this fact at our own peril.

Since many people are put off by language that seems for another age, and have no feeling for a spiritual process that seems to be clothed in the language of medieval mystics, it may be good to recall the acute analysis which Kierkegaard made of life's stages, beginning with *the aesthetic* which is preoccupied *with immediacy and pleasure,* progressing through *boredom* to *the ethical stage* which is characterized by *devotion to duty,* and then *ushered by humor* into the *religious stage which is characterized by radical faith,* or as Kierkegaard colourfully describes it, treading water seventy fathoms deep.

Or, similarly, in the psychological world, the way Erik Eriksson has sketched the different stages of the psychic growth. *These stages belong to secular knowledge* and make *a claim to be scientific.* Anyone who is serious about happiness and fulfillment can easily correlate them with whatever self-knowledge he or she possesses at any given time.

I believe that the pattern of human life and spiritual growth can be profitably conceived as a spiral. This spiral does not go directly upwards, but lies on its side. At the beginning, the coils of the spiral are small, but they get larger and larger as the spiral proceeds. There is no end to this spiral because when the coils get to be very large, we lose sight of the spiral's end.

The image of the spiral is helpful in that there is a place on it for all the negative and positive moments of life-growth. It has place for security and self-knowledge, for anxiety and fear, for hope and trust, for confusion and darkness, for a sunny feeling of the presence of love, to prolonged darkness and depression, to the feeling of being abandoned by God - lost in the dark night with no hope of light to guide the way.

The spiral has the possibility of showing the ever growing number of people on 12-step programs - for alcoholism, anorexia, bulimia, narcotics, pedophilia, gambling and other addictions or compulsions - that even though their higher power at the beginning of recovery is impersonal, or less than personal, that it is possible to come to a glimpse of a power that is not only personal but also loving. It can also teach them that there is something beyond *stoic abstinence, sheer plòd* and *the stage of the white-knuckled addict.*

It is helpful to keep this spiral in mind as it took shape in the life of one person who was dear to many, but who was very ordinary.

> When true simplicity is gained,
> To bow and to bend we shan't be ashamed
> To turn, turn will be our delight
> Till by turning, turning we come round right.

My mother's spiral began as the tiny end of a wire, and just as it goes around in the first tiny spiral that is never closed... but always open to a new and larger spiral that will lead on to the next… and someday disappear from our sight.

We think it is in our hands, and we have to act as if it were, but we come to the wisdom that it is always in other hands - and by *turning, turning we come round right.* The tiny end of the spiral will be left in our hands, but someday its gyrating coils will be out of our sight. It will have become too rich and strong to be entrusted to us anymore.

*　*　*　*

Lá an Luain

For Margaret McFadden

What a day you'll have
When all life's kindnesses are remembered:

The jugs of water on a parching morning,
The mugs of buttermilk,

The rising at night to tend the sick,
The race over the fields to ease the fevered,

The seeing of children into life,
The bathing of the dead,

The smile accepting us and all we are,
The welcome in to friend and stranger.

- Pádraig J. Daly, OSA